The Guide you have

Now you can tell w

In Edinburgh you will be greet ... es in the waiting lounge.

In South Yorkshire you can win a massage on a fruit machine.

In Derby, the ladies dress in different thematic costumes from week to week. Outfits have included dressing as French Maids, Schoolgirls, Nurses, Policewomen, with Caribbean wrap-around dresses, with Chinese Silk dresses, as Catwomen, even during Euro '96 as Footballers.

In Bristol, London & Middlesex there are parlours with a ceritable United Nations of masseuses with ladies from as many as 6 different countries, from Europe, the Far East, Africa & the Americas working at each establishment.

In Manchester there exists a parlour where all the ladies working there have model figures and hardly any would look out of place in a Miss World competition.

In Glasgow the massage rooms feature large circular beds and fully mirrored walls & ceilings to cater for the disabled.

In Bristol and Hove there are two cases of two apparently different establishments which are in fact one stretching between two blocks.

In Luton and Hove to minimise embarrassment for customers and masseuses, a photographic portfolio of ladies is available for the client's perusal.

In Hertfordshire there is a very attractive lady in a parlour who will serenade her clientele if so required.

First published in 1996 by McCoy's Guides,
P.O.Box 243, Telford, Shropshire, TF2 9WL

Cover Design: Origin Studios Ltd., Stoke on Trent
Printing and binding: Cox & Wyman Ltd., Reading

CONTENTS

INTRODUCTION

The ancient art of massage would appear to be becoming an ever more popular method of relaxation in our society. In most local papers and adsheets, adult magazines, contact magazines and in practically every public phone box in central London there are countless advertisements placed by female masseuses offering a wide variety of intriguing sounding services. Even the national press has got in on the act. The Daily Sport lists the telephone numbers of over 300 masseuses from Aberdeen to Plymouth - and that's just on a quiet day.

So where do you start to make a choice? And what can you expect for your money? You can start by investing in a phone call - but, invariably, and especially if it's a mobile number - you will find yourself paying for the pleasure of listening to a message asking you to call back later. If you do happen to get through, one of two things will happen. Either you will find yourself talking to the advertiser or her 'maid', and can expect to listen to an impossibly flattering description of your prospective masseuse's physical attributes. Or you will discover that you have rung a massage parlour.

In the former case, you prospective masseuse will suggest that you find your way to a phone box near her place of work, and ring her again. In many instances when you do so, you will find yourself listening to another message - which means that either she is occupied with another customer, or out. If she happens to be in, and is available for employment, you will be directed to a private address where you will almost certainly find a woman who bears little resemblance to the woman described over the phone. At that point you have the choice of staying for a massage, or leaving - usually with a volley of abuse ringing in your ears.

The alternative to this pot-luck (which might be better described as 'no-luck') system is to visit a massage parlour - an increasingly familiar sight in urban streets throughout Britain (often described simply as 'saunas' or 'health studios'). But which one, and where? All parlours have people employed to answer the phone and describe the services and facilities. These individuals are generally skilled in the art of salesmanship, and if you believe everything you hear you might reasonably expect to be visiting the most luxurious massage establishment, with the most beautiful masseuses, in the Western

Hemisphere. You will be given a glowing description of the facilities and services, and assured that there is no better value for money outside the finest fleshpots of South East Asia.

All too often, when you arrive at this impressive-sounding establishment you will find yourself standing outside a dingy shopfront, in a seedy street, in a part of the world that bears about as much resemblance to the description as Coronation Street does to Mayfair. Next, you will learn that nearly all massage parlours operate a shut door policy. In other words you will find yourself standing between an outer and inner door where you will have to signal your presence by ringing a bell. You will then be observed either through a spy-hole or by a remote TV camera. If you are not judged to be an undesirable (viz. drunk, football hooligan, regular time-waster or massage parlour researcher) you will be admitted, and given a 'menu' of various massage services ranging from 'standard' to 'V.I.P.' In some cases you may be able to make your selection of masseuse before you part with your money. In others despite telephone assurances to the contrary, you will find yourself back in pot-luck territory. Thereafter, the procedure is much the same in every establishment - shower, or jacuzzi, or sauna (or all three), recline on the massage table, choose an application of oil or talc, and enjoy your massage*.

So, how best do you establish what is fact and what is fiction in the wealth of establishments offering massage facilities? This guide is your best bet. Designed to take the guesswork out of choosing a massage parlour, it will provide you with all the information you might expect to receive (after suitable interpretation) from the management - and a great deal more. Where credit is due - for facilities, cleanliness, value, choice, quality etc. it is duly given. Where there is clearly room for improvement, we say so. In every case, our purpose remains the same: we intend to provide an objective, honest and accurate appraisal of every massage parlour featured. In so doing, we hope to raise the standards of a flourishing industry which - at its best - offers a valuable and pleasurable service to thousands of men and women every day throughout the country.

(* It has been rumoured that in some cases, masseuses have been known to offer sexual services in addition to a standard massage. With no personal experience of such activity, the publishers could not possibly comment.)

HOW TO USE

Most of the information listed in this guide is self-explanatory. The name, address and telephone number hardly need any explanation. The opening hours, unless the establishment is open 24 hours a day, are always from a time between 9 a.m. and 4 p.m. to a time between 5 p.m. and 6 a.m. The basic cost of massage is the lowest price quoted. Prices vary from time to time, so although correct now they may well have changed by the time you read this. Please check by phone before visiting the premises. Extras, e.g. Use of sauna, jacuzzi etc. would lead to a higher price. If credit cards can be used, this is indicated after the basic cost.

A= Access. V= Visa. A.E.= American Express. D.C.= Diner's Club.

My initial star rating is your principle indication of how good the establishment is.

☆ = Poor. ☆☆ = Average. ☆☆☆ = Good.
☆☆☆☆ = Very Good. ☆☆☆☆☆ = Outstanding.

My ratings (A,B,C,D) system is as follows. All are marks out of ten. A is for appearance. For example, Miss World entrants would rate 10. B is for behaviour and performance. Unfortunately I have only been able to indulge in a massage at a minority of the establishments listed, though I am beginning to get some feedback from people who have bought the first guide, so from my limited experience, plus theirs I am beginning to give more establishments a B rating, but many are still left blank.

C is for convenience of access. 10 would mean you can park securely on the premises. In central London, where parking is difficult, higher ratings tend to relate to the proximity of tube stations. Finally D is decor and facilities. The more tasteful and extensive they are, the higher the rating.

Appearance descriptions are based on at least one and often more than one visit to each establishment, together with verbal descriptions elicited from the establishment. Car parking or Tube Station notes are based on personal experience and the notes on numbers of ladies indicate how many ladies one is liable to find at any one time and the total number of ladies the management keep on their books. Finally the facilities notes indicate what one is likely to find for ones use besides the massage provided by the ladies.

The guide comes in basically 3 sections. First England, secondly Scotland and finally Wales. Within each country, the entries are listed alphabetically by county. England starts with Avon and ends with Wiltshire. Within each county, the entries are listed alphabetically by town or city and within each town or city, alphabetically by name of parlour.

At the beginning of each county there is a brief article about the parlours of that particular area. This gives you some idea as to which are the best establishments, as per my taste, which is the conventional one of finding that I enjoy a massage more from young, slim, yet shapely ladies. If however your taste is different please scan the book for what you are looking for. There are parlours with ladies to suit every taste listed here.

Part 1. England

AVON

Avon is really just another name for Bristol - an appropriately named city with a healthy population of generously breasted masseuses working in 16 different establishments. To be more accurate, there are actually only 15 establishments - two, somewhat confusingly, proving to operate from the same premises with the same staff.

When I left Club X, having made my usual notes about staff, decor and facilities, I moved on to a neighbouring parlour around the block - the imaginatively named No.38 (operating from No. 38 Jamaica St.) Having rung the door bell, I heard the sound of footsteps followed by a vigorous waggling of the door handle from the inside. The footsteps then retreated and assuming that a key was being fetched, I waited for a few minutes - to no avail. So I rang the bell again, and was eventually greeted by a rich West Country brogue saying: "You've already seen us. We're the same as round the block." Our conversation ended there. To this day I have absolutely no idea why the same premises are operating as two different businesses, with two different addresses, two different phone numbers, but with exactly the same staff. Perhaps it has something to do with an elaborate accounting procedure - or perhaps the management believes that two names, and two entrances are better than one.

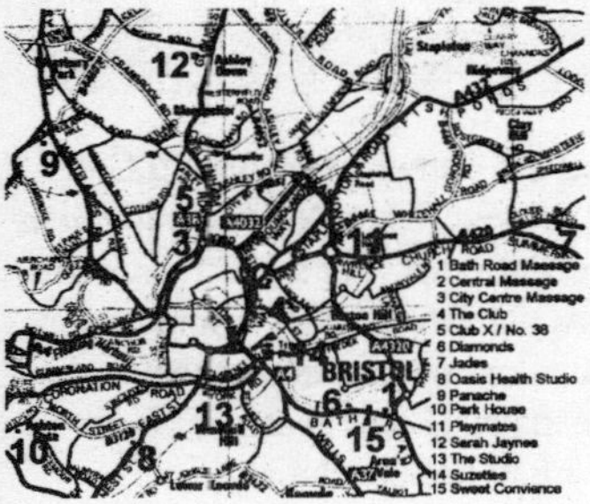

The waiting lounge at The Studio

The premier establishment in Bristol is The Studio, very professionally run by a young lady called Maria who is very approachable if you require any unusual type of massage. The staff are all young and include ladies from Brazil, Thailand, Egypt, Portugal, Hungary & Ghana - a regular United Nations. Unusual popular features include a rocking chair, mirrored ceilings in most though not all rooms & a waterbed. For sheer enthusiasm and a zest for work this establishment takes some beating - and not just in the West Country.

Unlike many similarly sized cities, like Birmingham for example, Bristol massage parlour staff do not dress uniformly. Some favour the ubiquitous clinical white coat, while a surprising number of others - no doubt feeling the tropical Severn Estuary heat - prefer to practice their craft in their underwear. The undergarment approach is conspicuously practised by four parlours close to the centre of the city - Central Massage, City Centre Sauna, The Club and Oasis Health Studio. All four have attractive staff, cheerfully disposed to their customers and fetchingly attired in very little. Central Massage, in particular, stood out as an unusually well appointed premises, with mirrored ceilings in several of the rooms, thereby giving any client a first class view of his masseuse at work.. Oasis should be noted also, however. The staff there are attractive and keen to assist in any way possible. One interesting feature there is a waterbed in one of the massage rooms. The Club, also with a fine looking bunch of ladies working there is currently about to undergo redecoration and a reorganization of the facilities available. One will be able to enjoy oneself there soon well and truly.

Left
A typical luxury room at Central Massage

Right
The waterbed room at Oasis

To the south-west of the city centre, just around the corner from Bristol City football club, is the Park House in Ashton Gate. This proved to employ three lovelier-than-usual masseuses, and an almost equally lovely receptionist. For some reason the latter takes great pains in emphasising that the staff are not Bristol girls - hinting that that is a quality to be particularly valued - and then goes on to caution that the establishment is closed on both weekends and Wednesdays. (I had heard of Never-on-a-Sunday, but Never-on-a-Wednesday is an anomaly I had not previously experienced).

In Arnos Vale, on Bath Road opposite HTV's palatial headquarters, is another of the better parlours in the city. At Bath Road Massage, I had one of the more interesting experiences during my Avon researches. Greeted at the door by a somewhat ample young lady, dressed only in her underwear, I was ushered into a lounge where three more women awaited. One was a slimmer version of the first, and similarly attired, a second was dressed casually in a blouse and jeans, and the third was rather formally attired in a business suit. Notwithstanding the fact the third was clearly interviewing the second with a view to prospective employment, all four appeared to be gratifyingly keen to offer me a massage. With other parlours to visit, I had to make regretful excuses and leave - having made a mental note to compliment them on their commendable enthusiasm. A more eager bunch of ladies it would be hard to imagine.

The St. Phillips area offers a venue - Suzette's - distinguished by their mature staff and correspondingly lower price. The remaining establishments in Bristol did not strike me as particularly noteworthy, although Playmates offers a fantasy room and Panache has some fairly attractive staff.

The only other town in Avon offering licensed massage facilities is Weston-Super-Mare, alma mater to the literary genius Lord Jeffrey Archer. There are just three parlours here, all clearly catering to a largely superannuated clientele. When I visited the busiest of the three, Boulevard, a retired 'major' type happened to arrive at the same time. Obviously a regular, he was greeted with effusive welcome by a buxom lass young enough to be his great granddaughter. There are no doubt worse ways of spending your retirement. Located above a bathroom fittings shop in a charming street lined with rows of beautiful pink cherry blossom trees, this is one of the more exclusively-situated parlours in Avon and the interior decor is more than equal to the location. Perhaps Lord Archer might find it a relaxing place to write his next novel.

BRISTOL - 0117

BATH ROAD MASSAGE ☆☆☆☆
387,Bath Rd., Arnos Vale Ratings A-7.B- .C-7.D-6.
Open 10 - 12. Tel.972 0310 Basic Cost. £15.
Appearance: Staff young and all sizes & races, cheerful and friendly.
Car Parking: Park outside or around the corner in Edward Rd.
Ladies:3 from 15 different. Facilities: Videos

CENTRAL MASSAGE ☆☆☆☆
54,Old Market St. Ratings A-7.B- .C-7.D-7.
Open 10-2. Tel.922 6944 Basic Cost £15.
Appearance: Staff varied in race & looks, but mainly young & attractive.
Car Parking: Park opposite.
Ladies: 3 from 15 different. Facilities: Sauna & Videos.

CITY CENTRE SAUNA ☆☆☆☆
39,Stokes Croft Ratings A-7.B- .C-4.D-7.
Open 10-4. Tel. 942 3072 Basic Cost £15.
Appearance: Staff young, racially varied & attractive.
Car Parking: Try and find a free meter or pay & display in York St.
Ladies: 3 from 23 different. Facilities: Sauna, Jacuzzi, Videos & Steam Room

The CLUB ☆☆☆☆
32/4, Midland Rd. Ratings A-8.B- .C-6.D-7.
Open 10-4. Tel. 927 3207 Basic Cost £15.
Appearance: Staff young, racially varied & attractive.
Car Parking: Park opposite on the road or in Kingsland Trading estate.
Ladies: 3 from 20 different. Facilities: Jacuzzi & Videos.

CLUB X ☆☆
57, Stokes Croft Ratings A-5.B- .C-4.D-6.
Open 24 hours a day. Tel. 924 5357 Basic Cost
Appearance: Staff of all ages, looks, races & sizes, some not unattractive.
Car Parking: Try and find a free meter or pay & display in York St.
Ladies: 2 to 7 from 15 different. Facilities: Sauna & Videos.

DIAMONDS ☆☆☆
363, Bath Rd., Arnos Vale Ratings A-6.B- .C-7.D-6.
Open Mon-Fri.11-11.Sat.12.30-11.Sun.2-10.Tel.977 4659 Basic Cost £10.
Appearance: Staff youngish, mainly slim and very versatile.
Car Parking: Park around the corner in Edward Rd.
Ladies: 3 from 13 different. Facilities: Jacuzzi, Videos, Fantasy room & Sunbed.

JADES ☆☆☆
22A,Bell Hill Rd., St. George Ratings A-5.B- .C-7.D-5.
Open Mon-Fri.11-12.Sat-Sun.3-10. Tel. 955 5373 .Basic Cost £8.
Appearance: Staff white, versatile and all ages & sizes.
Car Parking: Park outside or around the corner in Marling Rd.
Ladies: 3 from 9 different. Facilities: Videos

NO. 38 ☆☆
38, Jamaica St. Ratings A-5.B- .C-4.D-6.
Open 24 hours a day Tel. 944 5849. Basic Cost.
Appearance: Club X stretches from Stokes Croft to Jamaica St.
Car Parking: This is merely the back entrance. See Above.
Ladies: See above Facilities: See above.

OASIS HEALTH STUDIO ☆☆☆☆
60,West St., Bedminster Ratings A-7.B- .C-6.D-5.
Open 10-4. Tel. 923 1745. Basic Cost. £15
Appearance: Staff young, all sizes races and ages.
Car Parking: Park opposite or around the corner in Sion Rd.
Ladies: 3 from 12 different. Facilities: Videos, Sunken Baths & Waterbed.

PANACHE ☆☆☆

3, Highland Cres., Clifton Ratings A-6.B- .C-5.D-5.

Open 10.30-10.30. Tel. 974 1433. Basic Cost.£7.

Appearance: Staff white, youngish, slimmish & not unattractive.

Car Parking: Park on or around the corner in Highland Square.

Ladies: 3 from 10 different. Facilities:

PARK HOUSE ☆☆☆☆

26, Ashton Rd., Ashton Gate Ratings A-8.B- .C-7.D-7.

Open 10.30-7.Mon,Tues,Thurs,Fri. Tel. 953 3039. Basic Cost. £10.

Appearance: Staff young, racially varied, slim & attractive.

Car Parking: Park down the road or around the corner in Wells St.

Ladies: 3 from 12 different. Facilities: Videos.

PLAYMATES ☆☆☆

174,Lawrence Hill Ratings A-5.B- .C-7.D-6.

Open 10-2. Tel.941 4561 Basic Cost.

Appearance: Staff racially varied and very versatile.

Car Parking: Use free car park around corner in Dulcie Rd.

Ladies: 2 to 4 from 10 different. Facilities: Sauna, Fantasy room & Videos.

SARAH JAYNE'S ☆☆☆

282,Gloucester Rd. Ratings A-6.B- .C-7.D-5.

Open 10.30 - 9.30. Tel 942 8292 Basic Cost. £7.

Appearance: Staff white, youngish, slimmish & not unattractive.

Car Parking: Park opposite. Premises on Top Floor.

Ladies: 2 from 8 different. Facilities: Videos.

The STUDIO ☆☆☆☆☆

11,Whitehouse St. Ratings A-8.B- .C-6.D-7.

Open 10 - 2. Tel. 923 1294 Basic Cost £10.

Appearance: Staff young, racially varied, very versatile and attractive.

Car Parking: Park outside or further down the street.

Ladies: 3 from 18 different. Facilities: Jacuzzi, Videos & Waterbed.

SUZETTES ☆☆

7,Victoria Rd., St. Philips Ratings A- 4.B- .C- 8.D-5.

Open Mon-Sat 10-10. Sun 2-10.Tel 977 4080. Basic Cost £5.

Appearance: Staff versatile, mature & all shapes, sizes & races.

Car Parking: Park around the corner in Midland Rd.

Ladies: 3 from 7 different. Facilities: Sauna

SWEET CONVENIENCE ☆☆☆
367, Bath Rd., Arnos Vale Ratings A-5.B- .C-8.D-8.
Open 10-2 Tel.907 7685 Basic Cost
Appearance: Staff youngish, versatile & racially varied.
Car Parking: Park in neighbouring Edward Rd.
Ladies: 4 from 25 different. Facilities: Sauna, Jacuzzi, Videos, Cable TV & Sunbed.

WESTON-SUPER-MARE - 01934

BOULEVARD ☆☆☆☆
36, The Boulevard Ratings A-7.B- .C-7.D-7.
Open 10-11. Tel. 613214 Basic Cost £5.
Appearance: Staff youngish, slim, attractive and very versatile.
Car Parking: Park opposite.
Ladies:2 from 12 different. Facilities: Sauna, Jacuzzi & Videos.

CACHET ☆☆☆
12, Baker St. Ratings A-7.B- .C-8.D-5.
Open Mon-Sat 12-8 Tel. 643300 Basic Cost £7.
Appearance: Staff white, all shapes & sizes, versatile & youngish.
Car Parking: Park opposite or around the corner in Jubilee Rd.
Ladies: 2 from 7 different. Facilities: Jacuzzi & Videos.

TIFFANY'S ☆☆☆
16, Orchard Place Ratings A-5.B- .C-6.D-5.
Open 10-7.30. Tel 612755 Basic Cost.
Appearance: Staff young, all shapes & sizes, versatile & racially varied.
Car Parking: Park opposite
Ladies: 3 from 8 different. Facilities: Videos.

BEDFORDSHIRE

For a small county, Bedfordshire has its fair share of massage parlours, though this only means five, two in the county town - Bedford and three in the largest town - Luton.

Bedford boasts Genevieve's in Tavistock St., north of the town centre and located over a Kentucky Fried Chicken outlet. The staff are young and personable and the reception lounge, while hardly tidy, has a refreshing lived-in feel to it. Bedford's other establishment - Visions - is much smaller with only one lady there at any one time. It is however clean and the staff are friendly.

Luton boasts three parlours. One is in a class of its own. Studio 118 at 118, New Bedford Rd. is unusual in a variety of ways. Firstly it doubles as a photographic studio. When one arrives, one is first asked politely whether you are there for photography or massage. Assuming it is the latter, you are then offered a cup of coffee or tea, while you leaf through a photographic portfolio of all the ladies who work there, those available on that particular shift being clearly identified.

Left
Studio 118

Right
Sasha in the Chinese Room at Studio 118

After you make your choice of masseuse, you then proceed to choose your massage room - one of three thematic rooms - the Garden room, the Chinese room and the Greek room. The staff include Orientals and at least one lady of Caribbean stock. An attractive blonde called Jenna is particularly to be recommended. The man who runs this establishment is a gentleman and a credit to the industry. Luton is most certainly a lucky town, maybe not in its football prowess, but most certainly in its provision of massage.

The other two parlours are much of a muchness, both Maxine's and Midnight Blue are closer to the town centre than Studio 118 and both boast saunas. Maxine's used to boast some foreign staff, but unfortunately they would have appeared to have left.

BEDFORD - 01234

GENEVIEVE'S ☆☆☆☆
65A, Tavistock St. Ratings A-7.B-6.C-7.D-6.
Open 10-11.30 Tel.353127 Basic Cost £10.
Appearance: Staff young, slim and moderately attractive.
Car Parking: Park outside in street or on opposite side nearer town centre.
Ladies: 3 from 10 different. Facilities: Sauna, Videos & Mirrored Walls.

VISIONS ☆☆☆
49A,Commercial Rd. Ratings A-6.B- .C-8.D-6.
Open Mon-Sat 1-7. Tel. 218771 Basic Cost £5.
Appearance: Staff youngish, friendly & not unattractive.
Car Parking: Park on other side of road. Entrance in Western St.
Ladies: 1 or 2 from 3 different. Facilities:

LUTON - 01582

MAXINE'S ☆☆
6,Stuart St. Passage Ratings A-5.B- .C-5.D-5.
Open 11-11. Tel.410800 Basic Cost £10.
Appearance: Staff young, white and slim, but not particularly attractive.
Car Parking: Park at either side of passage - in Wellington St. or King St.
Ladies: 2 from 14 different. Facilities: Sauna & Jacuzzi.

MIDNIGHT BLUE ☆☆
9, Guildford St. Ratings A-5.B- .C-5.D-6.
Open 11-2. Tel.459179 Basic Cost.
Appearance: Staff young, racially varied & slim, but not classy.
Car Parking: Park around the corner in John St.
Ladies: 2 from 10 different. Facilities: Sauna

STUDIO 118 ☆☆☆☆☆
118,New Bedford Rd. Ratings A-8.B-8.C-10.D-8.
Open 10-10. Tel.480524 Basic Cost £20.
Appearance: Staff of all races, shapes & sizes. Mostly young and almost all attractive.
Car Parking: Park in grounds by building. Entry off Gregories Close.
Ladies: 4 or 5 from 17 different. Facilities: Sauna, Jacuzzi & Steam Room.

BERKSHIRE

Royal Berkshire while well endowed with racecourses & stately homes for the royals is not so well equipped with massage parlours - I have been able to find just one, the imaginatively named 613 Club at 613, Oxford Rd. Well equipped, tastefully decorated and with a healthy attractive range of ladies working there.

READING - 0118

The 613 Club ☆☆☆☆☆
613, Oxford Rd. Ratings A-7.B- .C-7.D-7.
Open 10-2. Tel. 956 0268 Basic Cost £20
Appearance: Staff young, slim, racially varied & attractive.
Car Parking: Park around the corner in Brock Gardens.
Ladies:3 from 15 different. Facilities: Sauna, Jacuzzis & Videos.

CAMBRIDGESHIRE

Unlike Oxfordshire, which has no massage parlours, this university county has three parlours, though none in the county town. Like most of the rest of East Anglia, the parlour situation is indeed parlous - only a limited number and with only a limited numbers of ladies working in them. None stand out.

PETERBOROUGH - 01733

STUDIO ONE ☆☆
230A,Lincoln Rd. Ratings A-5.B- .C-7.D-5.
Open Mon-Fri 11-7. Tel. 319292 Basic Cost £10.
Appearance: Staff not unattractive but hardly young
Car Parking: Park next door outside Iceland.
Ladies:1 lady. Facilities: Videos

ST.NEOTS - 01480

STUDIO ONE ☆☆
40,St.Mary's St., Eynesbury Ratings A-4.B- .C-8.D-7.
Open Mon-Fri 11-5.30 Tel. 471439 Basic Cost
Appearance: Staff cheerful and slimmish but older than average
Car Parking: Park outside or opposite.
Ladies: 1 from 3 different. Facilities: Sauna

WISBECH - 01945

HARMONY STUDIOS ☆☆☆
Unit 6, Grassgate Lane Ratings A-5.B- .C-9.D-7.
Open Mon-Sat 10.30 - 6.30 Tel. 474993 Basic Cost: £25
Appearance: Staff friendly and cheerful, but neither young nor shapely.
Car Parking: Industrial unit on N.E. fringe of town. Park on premises.
Ladies: 1 lady. Facilities: Sauna and Jacuzzi.

CHESHIRE

Cheshire is not a county one readily associates with massage, but it is quite well served for a county of its size. Crewe is the town that stands out with 4 parlours, two of which have well-deserved 4 star status. But the county town - Chester has three and Warrington also has a notable establishment whose staff also work at one of Manchester's better establishments - the Director's Lodge. Perhaps, the less said about Macclesfield's parlour the better.

The parlours of Crewe are fairly basic but in two of them one is served by some very attractive ladies. Fantasia located over a shop in Nantwich Rd. and with only one lady working there at a time is fairly basic as regards facilities, but the ladies, tastefully dressed in their underwear, are a delight. At Brooklyn's Sauna also in Nantwich Rd., there are now two ladies with two massage rooms both tastefully decorated. The girls vary but include as attractive ladies as one will find anywhere.

The gymnasium area at Kellie's.

At Warrington, is located the most extensive gymnasium I have seen in a small sauna anywhere in the country. The girls are quite delightful too, all young and shapely, some very attractive with one who is half-Indian and half-Spanish.

Chester & neighbouring Clwyd seem to specialize in parlours over cafes catering to the travelling public. In fact the parlour at Broughton is over the border in Wales, though its postal address is Chester, so two North Wales parlours - Champers at Broughton & Finesse at Bagillt have this curious type of location. Champers is pretty basic though it does feature the only fantasy room in Cheshire, but the girls are decidedly better looking than average, with a very tasty looking young Italian lady, in particular.

CHESTER - 01244

CHAMPERS ☆☆☆☆

Above the Big Breakfast Café, Main Rd., Broughton Ratings A-7.B- .C-9.D-6.
Open 12-9. Tel. 661327 Basic Cost £10
Appearance: Staff young, versatile, and racially varied, inc. ladies from both Italy & Brazil.
Car Parking: Park in restaurant car park.
Ladies:1 or 2 from 6 different. Facilities: Videos, sunbed & fantasy room.

DREAMS ☆☆

Unit 13, Babbage Rd., Factory Rd., Sandycroft. Ratings A-5.B- .C-8.D-5.
Open 11.30 - 8.30 Tel. 537171 Basic Cost £10
Appearance: Staff racially varied, versatile & youngish. One Brazilian.
Car Parking: On industrial estate. Park outside.
Ladies: 1 or 2 from 6 different. Facilities: Videos

MELANIES ☆☆☆
45A,Faulkner St., Hoole Ratings:A-6.B- .C-7.D-6.
Open Mon-Fri 12-10.Sat-Sun 12-9. Tel.313460 Basic Cost £10.
Appearance: Staff white, young & shapely. One Dutch.
Car Parking: Use nearby free car park. Entrance off Walker St.
Ladies:1 from 6 different. Facilities: Videos.

CREWE - 01270

ACAPULCO ☆☆
65,Edelston Rd. Ratings:A-3.B- .C-7.D-4.
Open 12-9. Tel. 256562 Basic Cost £5
Appearance: Staff white, all ages, shapes & sizes, some versatile.
Car Parking: Park around the corner in Cam St., where entrance is at rear.
Ladies:2 from 7 different. Facilities:

BROOKLYN'S SAUNA ☆☆☆☆
133, Nantwich Rd. Ratings:A-7.B-7.C-6.D-7
Open 12-9 Tel. 215600 Basic Cost
Appearance: Staff racially varied, versatile, all shapes & sizes & generally attractive.
Car Parking: Park at rear off Brooklyn St. or across road in Ernest St.
Ladies: 2 from 12 different. Facilities: Sauna

EXCELL ☆☆☆
211A,Nantwich Rd. Ratings:A-6.B- .C-6.D-6.
Open Mon-Sat 12-9.Sun 12-8. Tel.250647. Basic Cost £10.
Appearance: Staff white, young & versatile.
Car Parking: Park in side street to the left of Post Office
Ladies:2 from 8 different. Facilities: Sauna.

FANTASIA ☆☆☆☆
62A,Nantwich Rd. Ratings:A-7.B- .C-6.D-7.
Open 12-9. Tel.583411 Basic Cost £5.
Appearance: Staff young, attractive, racially varied & versatile.
Car parking: Park around the corner in Chambers St.
Ladies:1 from 7 different. Facilities:

MACCLESFIELD - 01625

ELITE HEALTH STUDIO ☆☆
84A,Mill St. Ratings:A-3.B- .C-3.D-6.
Open 11.30 - 9. Tel.611001 Basic Cost £10.
Appearance: Staff mainly white, versatile, & all shapes, sizes & ages. One Arabic.
Car Parking: Difficult - suggest you use car park in Duke St.
Ladies:1 from 7 different. Facilities: Sauna

WARRINGTON - 01925

KELLIE'S ☆☆☆☆☆

27,Church St. Ratings:A-8.B- .C-6.D-8.

Open Mon-Fri 11-9.Sat-Sun 12-9. Tel.244297 Basic Cost £10.

Appearance: Staff young, shapely and attractive.

Car Parking: Park further down the street on opposite side.

Ladies:2 from 5 different. Facilities: Sauna and gymnasium.

DERBYSHIRE

Although the north of the county has a curious lack of parlours, none in Buxton, Chesterfield or Matlock for example, south Derbyshire is as well supplied as many more urban counties. Indeed Derbyshire could be said to be blessed with one of the most enterprising parlours in the whole country.

Strangely, the town with the most establishments is not the city of Derby but Robert Lindsey's home town - Ilkeston. There, close to the Nottinghamshire border are four parlours. Adam & Eve is clean, tidy and well run with attractive staff, sauna and jacuzzi. It shares staff with Nero's in Huthwaite just over the border in Nottinghamshire, and as such has the same high standards as its sister establishment.. Ilkeston Sauna is lavishly equipped but the staff are hardly in the first flush of youth. Peaches Health Spa has young attractive staff and a sauna but little else to recommend it. Much the same can be said for A Touch of Class.

No, the place with the most distinctive establishments is the city of Derby. Aquarius Health Spa, which apparently keeps changing its name between the various signs of the Zodiac has some attractive staff who are fairly young and attend one dressed either as French maids or schoolgirls.

Left
Tinkerbell and
Georgie enjoying a
jacuzzi at Bubbles

Right
Thre catwomen
relaxing at Bubbles

The establishment that takes the cake is however Bubbles Health Spa, just opposite the station. Like Aquarius they dress thematically from week to week. When

I called they were dressed as Caribbean maidens with wrap-around skirts adorned with bananas and pineapples, but they have also dressed up as nurses, policewomen and come Euro '96 had plans for being dressed as footballers. They also cater particularly for the disabled and uniquely among the parlours I have visited offer a 10% discount to Unison members, something, I am sure, Rodney Bickerstaffe would appreciate. Given their proximity to the station I was not surprised when they indicated they had taken care of a few M.P.s in their time. Its location just opposite the station is so convenient.The enterprise of the manageress, Debbie, is something special to behold and is a credit to the city.

Other than those listed above Derbyshire has only three more parlours, one each in Long Eaton, Sandiacre & Ripley. The Long Eaton establishment has some attractive young staff but little else to recommend it, the less said about Riverside Sauna in Sandiacre the better. Elite sauna in Ripley has apparently improved of late.

Derby used, in addition, to have an establishment called St.Trinians, perhaps the origin of Derby's unique tradition of costumed staff, but alas the establishment closed down some time ago, so I am unable to report on it.

DERBY - 01332

AQUARIUS HEALTH SPA ☆☆☆☆
7/10, Brick St. Ratings:A-7.B- .C-9.D-6.
Open Mon-Thurs 10-10.Fri-Sat 10-12.Sun 11-7. Tel.297287. Basic Cost £15.
Appearance: Staff presentable, black and white & attractive.
Car Parking: Park outside or around the corner in Friargate.
Ladies: 3 from 10 different. Facilities: Sauna, Jacuzzi & Videos.

BUBBLES HEALTH SPA ☆☆☆☆☆
31/32,Railway Terrace Ratings:A-8.B- .C-7.D-7.
Open Mon-Thurs 10-11.Fri-Sat 10-10.Sun 12-10. Tel. 297943. Basic Cost £18.
Appearance: Young attractive staff. One lady Asian.
Car Parking: Park around the corner in Midland Rd.
Ladies: 4 from 12 different. Facilities: Sauna & Jacuzzi.

ILKESTON - 0115

ADAM & EVE ☆☆☆☆
53, Granby St. Ratings:A-7.B- .C-9.D-6.
Open 11-9. Tel.930 0396. Basic Cost £15 A/V.
Appearance: Staff youngish, racially varied & presentable.
Car Parking: Park in front.
Ladies: 3 from 10 different. Facilities: Sauna & Jacuzzi.

ILKESTON SAUNA ☆☆☆
12, Burr Lane Ratings:A-6.B- .C-10.D-8.
Open Mon-Fri 11-10.Sat 11-6. Tel.932 1466. Basic Cost £12.
Appearance: Staff versatile & all ages, sizes and races.
Car Parking: Park on premises.
Ladies: 3 from 8 different. Facilities: Sauna & Jacuzzi.

PEACHES HEALTH SPA ☆☆☆
62,Station Rd. Ratings:A-6.B- .C-9.D-5.
Open Mon-Fri 11-9.Sat 11-7. Tel.930 0824. Basic Cost £15.
Appearance: Staff racially varied and youngish.
Car Parking: Park in front.
Ladies: 2 or 3 from 6 different. Facilities: Sauna

TOUCH OF CLASS ☆☆☆
136 Nottingham Rd Ratings:A-6.B- .C-9.D-6.
Open Mon-Sat 1.30-9.30 Tel.944 7277 Basic Cost £15.
Appearance: Staff white, versatile and all ages, sizes & shapes.
Car Parking: Park in front.
Ladies:3 from 6 different. Facilities: Sauna

LONG EATON - 0115

G.B.HEALTH STUDIO ☆☆☆
22-24 Clay St. Ratings:A-6.B- .C-7.D-5.
Open Mon-Fri 11-9. Tel 973 6031 Basic Cost £15.
Appearance: Staff youngish, white, slim & presentable.
Car Parking: Park outside or up the street.
Ladies: 2 from 5 different. Facilities: Sauna

RIPLEY - 01773

ELITE MASSAGE ☆☆☆
4, Nottingham Rd. Ratings:A-5.B- .C-5.D-6.
Open 11-10. Tel. 512661. Basic Cost £15.
Appearance: Staff white, youngish & in beach wear in the summer.
Car Parking: Use Pay & Display in Butterley Hill.
Ladies: 2 or 3 from 8 different. Facilities: Sauna, Jacuzzi & Sunbed.
N.B. The above parlour has changed hands recently. Assessment is based on situation earlier this year and could well have changed for the better.

SANDIACRE - 0115

RIVERSIDE SAUNA ☆☆

4, Station Rd. Ratings:A-4.B- .C-9.D-6.

Open Mon-Fri 11-8.Sat 11-5. Tel. 939 6292 Basic Cost:£12

Appearance: Staff white, slim but distinctly older than average.

Car Parking: Use free council car park at rear off Bridge St.

Ladies: 2 ladies. Facilities: Sauna & Steam Cabinet.

DEVON

Devon only boasts four parlours - Christine's and Exeter Aroma in Exeter are pretty basic, though the one lady at Exeter Aroma is young and fit.

The one establishment in Plymouth has rather more to offer. Studio Two in Keyham St. has two or three ladies to choose from plus first class facilities including Sauna, Sun Capsule and a Hot Steam Tub. Ladies are also available for outcall massages and are a generally friendly bunch of ladies.

EXETER - 01392

CHRISTINE'S ☆☆☆

94B, Sidwell St. Ratings:A-6.B- .C-7.D-5.

Open Mon-Sat 10.30 - 9.30. Tel.499160. Basic Cost

Appearance: Staff all races, ages & sizes.

Car Parking: Park opposite. 94B is beyond the roundabout really in Blackboy Rd.

Ladies: 2 from 5 different. Facilities:

EXETER AROMA ☆☆☆

22, New Bridge St. Ratings: A-6.B- .C-4.D-5.

Open Mon-Fri 1-10. Tel.425828 Basic Cost £20.

Appearance: Staff young, slim & not unattractive.

Car Parking: Park further up the hill in Fore St. or in neighbouring car park

Ladies: One lady. Facilities:

PLYMOUTH - 01752

STUDIO TWO ☆☆☆☆

198B, Keyham Rd. Ratings:A-6.B- .C-5.D-7.

Open Mon-Sat 10-2.Sun.11-12. Tel.559955. Basic Cost £16 A/V.

Appearance: Staff racially varied, young & presentable.

Car Parking: Park in front or around the back

Ladies: 2 or 3 from 11 different. Facilities: Sauna, Sun Capsule & Hot Steam Tub.

TORQUAY - 01803

TORQUAY STUDIO ☆☆

Rear of 288, Union St Ratings:A-5.B- .C-5.D-5.

Open: Mon-Fri 11.30-7.30. Sat 11.30-6.30 Tel. 212044. Basic Cost £20

Appearance: Staff youngish & racially varied.

Car Parking: Access at rear of local pharmacy. Park opposite.

Ladies: 1 from 2 different. Facilities:

EAST SUSSEX

From the massage point of view East Sussex means Brighton or rather Hove. Indeed curiously, Hove has all the parlours in East Sussex with none in its supposedly more raunchy neighbour Brighton. And there are indeed some very distinctive parlours in this, the South-East's premier seaside resort area.

Like Bristol, Hove boasts a back to back establishment, with front & rear entrances, two names, addresses & phone numbers. The two names used here are Angel's Delight & Top to Toe. On this occasion I was not as surprised as I had been in Bristol. Here they were clearly on either side of a block and they were getting their phone numbers somewhat mixed up in the press. Here I was cheerfully admitted at the front and rear entrances, but on seeing the same girls, I realised I was wasting both my time and theirs. Not that the girls were unattractive, with as many as seven to choose from there are ladies to satisfy any taste.

The other distinctive establishment is Ambassador's Sauna & Massage located in Portland Rd. Distinctive because, like Studio 118 in Luton they use a photographic portfolio to show customers the various ladies & unlike Studio 118 the massage rooms as well. All in all a very professional parlour. The proprietor, I hear, is thinking of opening a second parlour in Worthing. Hopefully, by the time I get round to my next guide, it will be up and running.

Little of relevance attaches to the other two parlours which are perfectly acceptable but nothing out of the ordinary.

HOVE - 01273

AMBASSADOR'S SAUNA & MASSAGE ☆☆☆☆☆

37,Portland Rd. Ratings:A-8.B- .C-6.D-8.

Open 12-10. Tel. 735673. Basic Cost £15 A/V/AE.

Appearance: Staff young, racially varied, shapely & attractive. One Thai.

Car Parking: Park outside in road.

Ladies: 2 from 14 different. Facilities: Sauna, Jacuzzi, Water-bed & Outdoor Massage.

ANGEL'S DELIGHT ☆☆☆☆
Basement Flat, 15, Waterloo St. Ratings:A-6.B- .C-6.D-7.
Open 10.30 - 9.30 Tel. 771737 Basic Cost £30.
Appearance: Staff versatile & all ages, races, shapes & sizes. One Spanish, one Swiss.
Car Parking: Park outside or in a neighbouring street.
Ladies: 2 to 7 from 14 different. Facilities: Sauna, Jacuzzi & Videos.

KITTEN'S SAUNA ☆☆☆
93A, Boundary Rd. Ratings:A-6.B- .C-5.D-5.
Open Mon-Sat 11.30-8.Sun 12-7. Tel. 422155 Basic Cost £15.
Appearance: Staff all shapes & sizes, young, white & versatile.
Car Parking: Park around the corner in Halliburton Rd. where entrance is.
Ladies: 2 or 3 from 12 different. Facilities: Sauna, Fantasy room & Videos.

TOP TO TOE ☆☆☆☆
37,Lower Market St. Ratings:A-6.B- .C-6.D-7.
Open 10.30-9.30 Tel.748499 Basic Cost £30.
Appearance : Angels Delight lies between Waterloo St. & Lower Market St. This is merely the rear entrance.
Car Parking: See Above.
Ladies: See Above. Facilities: See Above.

VENUS HEALTH STUDIO ☆☆☆
2,Brunswick Rd. Ratings:A-6.B- .C-6.D-6.
Open Mon-Sat 11-9. Tel. 737537 Basic Cost £15.
Appearance: Staff young, white, shapely & versatile.
Car Parking: Park in Brunswick Rd. or some nearby street.
Ladies:1 from 5 different Facilities: Videos.

EAST YORKSHIRE

East Yorkshire or North Humberside as it was known for a while does not boast as many parlours as one might have expected. The other parts of Yorkshire are well endowed, but I could only find three parlours here. Unfortunately, I was not well received at Studio Spin in Bridlington. The staff there are very attractive, but at the door, they seemed more concerned with relieving me of the basic massage charge of £10 than of offering me particularly good service. The 621 Studio has young and generally attractive staff but the premises are small & while obviously well established the decor did not strike me as anything particularly distinctive.

Victoria and the jacuzzi at Mystique

The same thankfully cannot be said of Mystique, a newly opened parlour on an industrial estate, which is tastefully decorated with top of the range facilities and from what I saw while there young attractive staff. Uniquely among the parlours I have visited it boasted a automatic snackbar with a first-class range of soft drinks and refreshments.

BRIDLINGTON - 01262

STUDIO SPIN ☆☆☆
10, West St. Ratings:A-6 .B- .C-9 .D-6 .
Open Mon-Fri 10.30-9.Sat 10.30-6. Sun 11-5. Tel.601928.Basic Cost £10.
Appearance: Staff youngish, versatile & racially varied.
Car Parking: Park opposite.
Ladies: 2 from 6 different. Facilities: Sauna

HULL - 01482

MYSTIQUE HEALTH & LEISURE ☆☆☆☆
Unit 1, Kingston Industrial Estate, Ropery St. Ratings:A-7.B- .C-9.D-7.
Open: 10-10. Tel.222244 Basic Cost £10 A/V
Appearance: Staff white, versatile and all ages, shapes & sizes.
Car Parking: On Industrial estate. Park by unit.
Ladies: 2 to 4 from 12 different. Facilities: Sauna, Jacuzzi, Sunbed, Amusement machine, Videos & Snackbar.

621 STUDIO ☆☆☆
621, Anlaby Rd. Ratings:A-5.B- .C-8.D-6.
Open Mon-Fri 11-9.Sat 11-7..Sun 12-6. Tel.566656. Basic Cost £8.
Appearance: Staff versatile, racially varied & all ages, shapes & sizes.
Car Parking: Park around the corner in Wheeler St.
Ladies:3 from 10 different. Facilities: Sauna & Videos.

ESSEX

The county of the famed Essex girls would, one feels, be the sort of place one would expect to find a plethora of parlours. After all your typical Essex girl would feel really at home easing the aches & pains of her Essex men. So, bearing that in mind,

Essex turns out to be somewhat of a disappointment. Only seven parlours, with three in the greater Southend area, but none in the other major towns of Chelmsford, Colchester, Harlow and Basildon.

With one exception, even these seven are hardly extremely notable. The parlours in the Southend area are all fairly non-descript, though Westcliff Sauna does boast an attractive French Caribbean lady and a blonde American. Over in Wickford is a more notable establishment, where a range of local lovelies operate from a parlour sited in the middle of a council house estate. Incongruously one has a commercial choice there of a convenience store, a laundrette & the Wickford Health Club, which while a pretty basic establishment boasts a sauna as well as videos and generally attractive staff.

The most notable parlour in Essex is however the Aquarius Health Spa in Waltham Abbey. Located in a quiet, at first sight domestic location, 9, Upshire Rd. boasts not only convenient on site parking, but a charming receptionist, attractive staff and a range of facilities second to none. In particular a most attractive heated swimming pool - one of only two in the entire country that I have come across. While it could be justifiably regarded as somewhat pricey, it is undoubtedly one of the smartest upmarket establishments I have come across in the entire South-East.

Finally, curiously located in the quiet commuter village of West Horndon, near Brentwood is Pampers, a pretty basic parlour, but one with some attractive staff who operate with a friendly and courteous manner towards all who call.

BILLERICAY - 01277

JULIE'S ☆☆☆

21,Cavell Rd. Ratings:A-7.B- .C-8.D-6.

Open Mon-Sat 12-8.30. Tel. 622937 Basic Cost £18.

Appearance: Staff youngish, white and not unattractive.

Car Parking: Park outside in the road.

Ladies: 2 from 12 different. Facilities: Sauna

BRENTWOOD - 01277

PAMPERS ☆☆☆☆

58, Station Rd., West Horndon Ratings:A-7.B- .C-5.D-7.

Open Mon-Fri 10-8.Sat 10-6. Tel. 811056 Basic Cost £10.

Appearance: Staff racially varied and all ages, shapes & sizes.

Car Parking: Park around the corner along Thorndon Rd.

Ladies: 2 from 10 different. Facilities: Sauna

LEIGH-ON-SEA - 01702

V.I.P.MASSAGE ☆☆☆

1107, London Rd. Ratings:A-6.B- .C-7.D-6.

Open Mon-Fri 10-10.Sat-Sun 10-7.Tel.480330. Basic Cost £15.

Appearance: Staff white, young & not unattractive.

Car Parking: Entrance off Cheltenham Drive. Park back along London Rd.

Ladies: 2 from 10 different. Facilities:

SOUTHEND-ON-SEA - 01702

ESSEX HEALTH & BEAUTY ☆☆☆

10,West St., Prittlewell Ratings:A-6.B- .C-8.D-6.

Open Mon-Fri 10-10.Sat-Sun 10-7. Tel.430800.Basic Cost £10.

Appearance: Staff youngish, white, some slim, some shapely.

Car Parking: Park at rear where entrance is.

Ladies: 2 from 10 different. Facilities:

WALTHAM ABBEY - 01992

AQUARIUS HEALTH SPA ☆☆☆☆☆

9, Upshire Rd. Ratings:A-8.B- .C-10.D-9.

Open Mon-Sat 11-10.Sun 12-9. Tel.764856. Basic Cost £40

Appearance: Staff versatile, white, attractive & young. One half-Egyptian.

Car Parking: Park on premises.

Ladies: 2 from 14 different. Facilities: Sauna, Jacuzzi, Sunbed & Swimming pool

WESTCLIFF-ON-SEA - 01702

WESTCLIFF SAUNA ☆☆☆

67D, Canewden Rd. Ratings:A-7.B- .C-6.D-6.

Open 11-10.30 Tel.330848 Basic Cost £10.

Appearance: Staff young, slim & racially varied.

Car Parking: Park around the corner in Hamlet Court Rd.

Ladies: 2 from 10 different. Facilities: Sauna

WICKFORD - 01268

WICKFORD HEALTH CLUB ☆☆☆☆

23, Appletree Way Ratings:A-7.B- .C-7.D-6.

Open Mon-Sat 10.30-8. Tel.761644 Basic Cost £10

Appearance: Staff white, slim, all ages, versatile & moderately attractive.

Car Parking: Park outside or opposite.

Ladies:2 from 6 different. Facilities: Sauna, Sunbed & Videos.

GREATER LONDON

A third of the parlours in the entire United Kingdom are located in just two counties - the two Greaters - London & Manchester. Both have over 50 establishments, including some of the best and the worst that the country offers.

Just as the distribution of parlours around the whole country is somewhat uneven, so is the distribution of parlours within Greater London. There are hardly any in West London, and not too many in South London. They seem to be concentrated in certain London boroughs. South of the river they appear to only exist in the Croydon, Lambeth, Streatham & Bexley areas. North of the river they cover virtually all of north, east and north-west London, plus the north-western & eastern suburbs.

Out in the suburbs the parlours are all fairly basic but there are some very attractive staff at Gants Hill Sauna in Ilford and Wembley Sauna, where one of the ladies working there is half-Egyptian. Both of these establishments have saunas and friendly receptionists, Gants Hill featuring an international range of attractive staff, with ladies from France, Thailand, Malaysia and the Czech Republic.

Cherry Orchard Beauty Clinic and Gemini Saunas in Crayford are also worthy of note, with attractive ladies working in both from time to time. Also to the south east is Bexley Sauna with a sauna and a jacuzzi and a first class selection of young ladies.

One parlour out in the suburbs does however stand out. That is Edgware Unisex Health & Beauty Centre in Edgware High St. The staff are young and attractive and are an entirely international range - the six ladies working there coming from Israel, Sweden, Thailand, Singapore, Austria & Poland - as good an advert for the United Nations as you could expect to find anywhere. Furthermore the premises are tastefully decorated and feature a steam room as well as a solarium.

In outer London - the 0181 part - there are a number of interesting parlours. If you are black or Asian forget about Anita's in High Rd., Leyton When I called there almost immediately after gaining entrance, the doorbell rang and one of the two tall not unattractive masseuses working there looked through the spyhole at the gentleman seeking a massage. After looking at him she turned to her colleague and exclaimed "It's a black". To which her friend replied "Tell him we're busy". The first duly did so, indicating they would only be free after a couple of hours. Actually since I then made my excuses and left, they had time galore on their hands.

Out at Chingford or to be precise at Higham's Park is a very interesting establishment. Higham's Park Sauna boasts an international staff with ladies from

London Central

1 Ace Suana
2 Affinity
3 Bel-Air
4 Beverly Hills Sauna
5 Bluebell's Massage
6 Blue Moon
7 Body One
8 College Sauna
9 Euston Sauna
10 First Class Sauna
11 Marble Arch Health Club
12 New Aquarius Sauna
13 New Experience
14 Omega Health Club
15 Paradise Sauna
16 Rainbow Health & Beauty
17 Steam & Sun
18 Tease Sauna
19 Top Class
20 Westminster Sauna
21 Willesden Sauna

London East

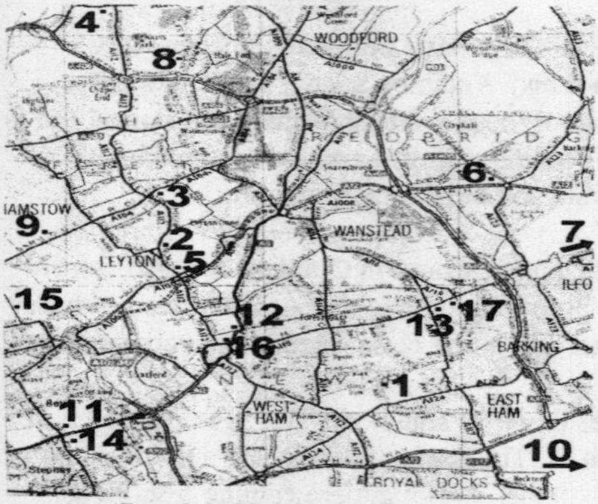

1 Angels Sauna
2 Anita's
3 Bakers Arms Sauna
4 Chingford Sauna & Solara
5 Cosmo's
6 Gants Hill Sauna
7 Goodmayes Health Club
8 Highmams Park Sauna
9 Lea Bridge Sauna
10 Mandy's
11 New City Sauna
12 New Elite Sauna
13 Park Sauna
14 Rumors
15 Solitaire
16 Stratfoed Sauna
17 Utopia Sauna
18 Wanstead Sauna Club

London North

Left
1 Adonis Sauna & Health Club
2 Aqua Sauna
3 Bay Sauna
4 Elite Harringay Sauna
5 Fantasy Sauna
6 Hornsey Sauna
7 Ishka Bath
8 Lanacombe Sauna
9 Sterling Sauna
10 Thai Sauna

London West

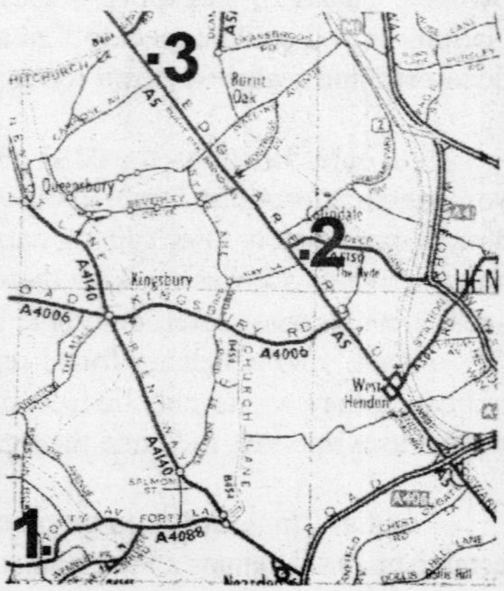

Right
1 Wembley Sauna
2 Colindale Sauna
3 Edgware Unisex Health & Beauty Centre

Poland, Thailand, Italy and America. You get to it having passed through a ground floor hair dressing salon and then ascending an outside staircase from a very attractive back garden. The rooms have unusual, yet distinctively attractive decoration, matching the excellent choice of ladies.

Left
A massage room at Cherry Orchard Beauty Clinic

Right
The King-sized jacuzzi at Solitaire

At Solitaire, formerly known as Roleks Health Club, are as attractive a range of young ladies as you will find anywhere else in London. The facilities are among the best I have seen in London and the staff are uniformly young & attractive including several Thai ladies. It boasts a pleasantly large scale jacuzzi and unusually they have one of the latest opening hours in the country. At 4p.m., just when most workers are thinking of calling it a day, they are opening up. On the other hand they do not close until 4a.m.

Left
The plunge pool at Angel's Sauna

Right
A massage room at Stratford Sauna

Also in the East End is Stratford Sauna, an establishment with an international staff - From the Far East and Caribbean, as well as English, including an enthusiastic young lady by the name of Amber who often doubles as a receptionist. Their most distinctive feature was an unusual system of introduction cards. When a gentleman had made his choice of lady for his massage, he simply handed the appropriate introduction card to the receptionist, thereby minimising any attendant embarassment to the ladies not selected - a system I have not found in any other parlour. Unfortunately they have recently decided to abandon this practice, but they are as friendly a bunch of ladies and management as you will find in any other London parlour.

Angels Sauna in Upton Park, just around the corner from West Ham United, has very distinctive facilities - in particular a lovely plunge pool as well as a sauna, steam room and sunbeds. The ladies are not bad looking either.

North London has a wide selection of parlours with a wide range of ladies from all over the world. Selections of ladies including many from the Far East can be found at Thai Sauna and Lanacombe Sauna. At Lanacombe there are as many as 11 ladies available at any one time including as wide a range of nationalities as you will find anywhere - ladies from Thailand, France, Germany, Poland, Russia & Brazil. Only its sister establishment Aqua Sauna in Holloway boasts more.

At Fantasy Sauna in Archway Rd., Highgate there are some attractive young ladies working there and a solarium and gymnasium as well as a sauna and video facilities, but curiously considering the name of the establishment, no fantasy room.

Streatham Sauna

Left
A massage room

Right
The gym

South of the river the establishment that stands out is Streatham Sauna, where there are two ladies generally available, both young and attractive. The parlour also boasts a large gym, plus decent-sized jacuzzi and sauna. Furthermore they accept Access and Visa.

Three further parlours are worthy of note, principally because of the friendly nature of the ladies working at each establishment. Sparkles in South Norwood has although only basic facilities, as friendly a bunch of ladies as you will find anywhere in the capital. Rumors in Bow has an international flavour with ladies from Singapore and France, and frankly among the most attractive ladies I have seen at any of the parlours in London. The establishment also boasts first-class facilities including sauna, jacuzzi and solarium. Lastly in Outer London one must mention Willesden Sauna, with again an international flavour, ladies here come from Greece, Italy and France. A basic parlour but with a friendly and attractive workforce.

In the Inner London - 0171- area, there are further interesting parlours - notably Aqua Sauna with more ladies on at any one time and from a bigger roster than anywhere else in the country. And there are very attractive ladies working at Beverley Hills Sauna, College Sauna where there is a very friendly receptionist, Omega Health Club & Steam and Sun. Omega almost matches Aqua by boasting not only a choice of 7 ladies available after 6p.m.,but a roster of 40 different ladies working there in all.

Bel Air in West Hampstead is one of the best equipped parlours in the nation's capital with sauna, jacuzzi, sunbeds and steam room. The staff are young & attractive including ladies from both France and Italy. Paradise is to be found in Neasden and the name is not too far off the truth, believe it or not.

The ladies at two more parlours are friendly and welcoming. Marble Arch Health Club has a young racially varied selection of staff, including ladies from both France and Germany. Just around the corner from Marble Arch, it is probably the best parlour in the West End. Tease Sauna in the east end of the city has a pleasant interior, though only the obvious sauna as an extra facility. The staff are however only too pleased to try and satisfy your every whim.

Two associated parlours with a classy bunch of ladies are to be found either side of the river - New Aquarius & Westminster Sauna - though only boasting basic facilities, also boast an attractive range of staff from Europe & the Far East in the case of New Aquarius and staff from the unusual collection of countries - Finland, Ireland, Brazil & Thailand in the case of Westminster.

BARNET - 0181

NEW BARNET SAUNA ☆☆

8, East Barnet Rd., New Barnet Ratings:A-5.B- C-6.D-5.

Open 11.30-10. Tel.440 9408 Basic Cost:£15

Appearance: Staff white, shapely, & mature, but over made up.

Car Parking: Park around the corner in Station Rd.

Ladies:2 from 10 different. Facilities: Sauna

BEXLEY - 01322

ANNALISE'S MASSAGE ☆☆☆

89A, High St. Ratings:A-6.B- .C-6.D-6.

Open Mon-Fri 11-8.Sat-Sun 11.30-7. Tel.557573. Basic Cost £10

Appearance: Staff white, young, versatile & slim. Two from down under.

Car Parking: Park around the corner in Albert or Thanet Rd.

Ladies:1 from 8 different. Facilities: Videos & Bubble bath.

BEXLEY SAUNA ☆☆☆☆
16,Bourne Rd. Ratings:A-7.B- .C-7.D-5.
Open 11-11. Tel.558699 Basic Cost £12.
Appearance: Staff racially varied, slim, tall & versatile.
Car Parking: Park around the corner in Thanet or Albert Rd.
Ladies:2 from 10 different. Facilities: Sauna & Jacuzzi.

CRAYFORD - 01322

GEMINI SAUNAS ☆☆☆☆
14,Station Rd. Ratings:A-7.B- .C-8.D-6.
Open 12-8. Tel.559509 Basic Cost £10.
Appearance: Staff youngish, all shapes & sizes, versatile and attractive, including ladies from Singapore and Portugal.
Car Parking: Park outside.
Ladies:1 from 6 different. Facilities: Sauna & Sunbed.

CROYDON - 0181

ANGELINES ☆☆☆
4,Bridge Parade, Waddon Rd. Ratings:A-5.B- .C-7.D-6.
Open Mon-Fri 11-9.Sat 12-7. Tel.681 2330. Basic Cost £18.
Appearance: Staff white, youngish, cheerful and all sizes.
Car Parking: Park around the corner in Benson Rd.
Ladies:2 from 10 different. Facilities: Sauna, Plunge pool & Steam room.

CHERRY ORCHARD BEAUTY CLINIC ☆☆☆☆
89A,Cherry Orchard Rd. Ratings:A-7.B- .C-6.D-6.
Open 11.30-9. Tel.681 6981 Basic Cost £10 A/V.
Appearance: Staff young, white, presentable & versatile.
Car Parking: Park outside, before 5 using pay and display.
Ladies:2 from 14 different. Facilities: Sauna & Sunbed.

DAGENHAM - 0181

CHEQUERS HEALTH STUDIO ☆☆☆
2,Chequers Parade Ratings:A-6.B- .C-7.D-5.
Open 12-11. Tel.592 4089. Basic Cost £10 A/V.
Appearance: Staff young, slim, racially varied & versatile.
Car Parking: Park around the corner in Goresbrook Rd.
Ladies:2 from 10 different. Facilities: Sauna & Sky TV.

EDGWARE - 0181

EDGWARE UNISEX HEALTH & BEAUTY CENTRE ☆☆☆☆
96,High St. Ratings:A-7.B- .C-4.D-7.
Open 10.30-9 Tel.952 5952 Basic Cost £12.
Appearance: Staff young & attractive, from Thailand, Israel, Sweden, Poland, Singapore & Austria
Car Parking: Park around the corner in Manor Park Cres.
Ladies:2 or 3 from 6 different. Facilities: Steam Room & Solarium.

ILFORD - 0181

GANTS HILL SAUNA ☆☆☆☆
5,Woodford Ave., Gants Hill Ratings:A-8.B- .C-7.D-7.
Open Sun-Thurs 11-11.Fri-Sat 11-12. Tel.550 6070. Basic Cost £15.
Appearance: Staff young, attractive & versatile, including ladies from the Czech Republic, France, Thailand & Malaysia.
Car Parking: Park in neighbouring streets.
Ladies:3 from 12 different. Facilities: Sauna & Sunbed.

GOODMAYES HEALTH CLUB ☆☆☆
16,Goodmayes Rd Ratings:A-6.B- .C-7.D-6.
Open 11-11. Tel. 599 8276 Basic Cost £11.
Appearance: Staff young, racially varied & versatile. One Italian.
Car Parking: Park around the corner in Goodmayes Ave.
Ladies:2 from 10 different. Facilities: Sauna & Jacuzzi.

INNER LONDON - 0171

ACE SAUNA
508,King's Rd.,SW10. Ratings:A- .B- .C-5.D-7.
Open Mon-Fri 11-1.30.Sat 11-12.30.Sun 11-12. Tel. 352 1872. Basic Cost £20 A/V.
Appearance: Money required up front. Racially varied staff include a New Zealander.
Car Parking: Park outside or around the corner in Slaidburn St.
Ladies:3 from 10 different. Facilities: Sauna, Spa pool, Solarium & Sky TV.

AQUA SAUNA ☆☆☆☆
42,Hornsey Rd.,Holloway,N7. Ratings:A-8.B- .C-7.D-6.
Open Mon-Sat 11-12.Sun 2-12. Tel.700 5393. Basic Cost £10.
Appearance: Staff young & slim including Thai, Polish and Asian ladies, plus one half-French, half-Russian.
Car Parking: Park around the corner in Ashburton Grove.
Ladies: 13 from 50 different. Facilities: Sauna Steam room, Bubble bath & Plunge pool.

BEL-AIR ☆☆☆☆☆
170,West End Lane, NW6 Ratings:A-8.B- .C-5.D-7.
Open 10.30-1.30 Tel.794 9747 Basic Cost £15.
Appearance: Staff white, young, attractive & shapely, inc. French & Italian ladies.
Car Parking: Park around the corner in Lymington Rd.
Ladies:2 from 10 different. Facilities: Sauna, Jacuzzi, Gym, Sunbed & Steam room.

BEVERLY HILLS SAUNA ☆☆☆☆
68,Caledonian Rd.,N1 Ratings:A-7.B- .C-5.D-7.
Open 12-12. Tel.837 6543 Basic Cost £10.
Appearance: Staff attractive, young & slim. One Brazilian, one French Caribbean.
Tube Station: Use King's Cross.
Ladies: 3 from 15 different. Facilities: Sauna & Jacuzzi.

BLUEBELL'S MASSAGE ☆☆☆
11,Charlotte Pl.,W1 Ratings:A-6.B- .C-3.D-7.
Open 11-12.. Tel.637 0150 Basic Cost £20.
Appearance: Staff all ages, shapes & sizes, including ladies from France, Sweden, Italy & Spain.
Tube Station: Use Goodge St.
Ladies: 4 from 10 different. Facilities:

BODY ONE
140, Marylebone Rd.,NW1 Ratings:A- .B- .C-7.D-8.
Open 10-12. Tel.486 5675. Basic Cost £24.
Appearance: Money required up front. Receptionist would only say staff very qualified.
Tube Station: Use Baker St.
Ladies: 2 from 6 different. Facilities: Sauna

COLLEGE SAUNA ☆☆☆☆
193, Royal College St.,NW1 Ratings:A-7.B- .C-5.D-6.
Open Mon-Sat 11-12.30.Sun 12-11.30. Tel. 485 5554 Basic Cost £12
Appearance: Staff young, slim, attractive including Brazilian & American ladies.
Tube Station: Use Camden Town
Ladies:2 from 10 different. Facilities: Sauna

EUSTON SAUNA & SOLARIUM ☆☆☆
58, Eversholt St.,NW1 Ratings:A-6.B- .C-4.D-7.
Open 11-11 Tel 383 3402 Basic Cost £15
Appearance: Staff youngish, slim & racially varied inc.ladies from Sweden and France.
Tube Station: Use Euston
Ladies: 4 from 12 different. Facilities: Sauna & sunbeds.

FIRST CLASS SAUNA ☆☆
180, Royal College St.,NW1 Ratings:A-5 B- .C-5 D-5.
Open Mon-Thurs 11-1.Fri 11-6. Tel.267 4709. Basic Cost £15.
Appearance: Staff all ages, shapes & sizes. Used by gays after 6 on Friday.
Tube Station: Use Camden Town
Ladies:2 to 4 from 10 different. Facilities: Sauna

HORNSEY SAUNA ☆☆☆
522, Hornsey Rd.,N19 Ratings:A-5.B- .C-8.D-6.
Open 11-11 Tel.281 2367 Basic Cost £10.
Appearance: Staff young & white including one Italian.
Car Parking: Park around the corner in Lambton Rd.
Ladies:2 from 12 different. Facilities: Sauna & Bubble bath.

MARBLE ARCH HEALTH CLUB ☆☆☆☆
3, Seymour Place, W1 Ratings:A-7.B- .C-5.D-5.
Open 11-1. Tel.724 1202. Basic Cost £20 AE.
Appearance: Staff young, slim, racially varied & attractive, including several Europeans.
Tube Station: Use Marble Arch.
Ladies: 3 from 14 different. Facilities: Sauna & Sunbeds.

NEW AQUARIUS SAUNA ☆☆☆☆
278,Grays Inn Rd.,WC1 Ratings:A-7.B- .C-5.D-6.
Open 11-9. Tel.833 8381 Basic Cost £10.
Appearance: Staff young, shapely & versatile inc. Thais, Chinese & various Europeans.
Car Parking: Park around the corner on meter in Frederick St.
Ladies: 2 from 10 different. Facilities: Sauna

NEW EXPERIENCE ☆☆
275, Eversholt St., NW1 Ratings:A-5.B- .C-4.D-5.
Open Mon-Fri 11-1.Sat-Sun 12-12. Tel.387 6441. Basic Cost £15.A/V/AE
Appearance: Staff racially varied, versatile, all sizes & ages, including a Brazilian lady.
Car Parking: Park on Pay & Display outside.
Ladies: 3 from 12 different. Facilities: Sauna & Sunbeds.

OMEGA HEALTH CLUB ☆☆☆☆
141-145, Kentish Town Rd., NW1. Ratings:A-7.B- .C-5.D-6.
Open 11-4. Tel.482 5538 Basic Cost £10.
Appearance: Staff young and slim including Thai, Indian, Chinese & European ladies.
Car Parking: Park around the corner on a meter in Kelly St.
Ladies:3 to 7 from 40 different. Facilities: Sauna & Steam Room.

RAINBOW HEALTH & BEAUTY ☆☆☆
428, Edgware Rd., W2 Ratings:A-6.B- .C-4.D-6.
Open 12.30-10. Tel.402 6499 Basic Cost £20.
Appearance: Staff young, shapely & not unattractive.
Tube Station: Use Edgware Rd.
Ladies: 3 or 4 from 7 different. Facilities: Bubble Bath

STEAM & SUN ☆☆☆☆
17-19, Chalton St., NW1 Ratings:A-7.B- .C-4.D-5.
Open 11-5. Tel. 387 0469. Basic Cost £15
Appearance: Staff young, shapely & attractive including ladies from Italy and Thailand.
Tube Station: Use Euston.
Ladies: 3 to 9 from 15 different. Facilities: Sauna, Sunbed, Steam Room & Sky TV.

TEASE SAUNA ☆☆☆☆
8, Great Eastern St., EC2 Ratings:A-7.B- .C-3.D-7.
Open Mon-Fri 11-9.30.Sat-Sun 12-8. Tel.247 5034. Basic Cost £15.
Appearance: Staff racially varied, versatile, generally attractive, all ages & sizes.
Tube Station: Use Liverpool St. or Shoreditch.
Ladies: 2 from 10 different. Facilities: Sauna.

TOP CLASS ☆☆☆
38, Chalk Farm Rd., NW1 Ratings:A-6.B- .C-5.D-7.
Open 12 - 2. Tel.267 9168 Basic Cost £15.
Appearance: Staff racially varied & slim including ladies from Norway, France & Spain.
Car Parking: Park on a meter around the corner in Ferdinand St.
Ladies: 2 from 12 different. Facilities: Sauna, Jacuzzi & Sunbeds.

WESTMINSTER SAUNA ☆☆☆☆
162, Westminster Bridge Rd., SE1. Ratings:A-5.B- .C-4.D-5.
Open 12-10. Tel.401 9001 Basic Cost £10 A/V
Appearance: Staff young & attractive inc. ladies from Thailand, Brazil, Finland & Eire.
Tube Station: Use Lambeth North.
Ladies: 2 from 10 different. Facilities: Sauna

OUTER LONDON - 0181

ADONIS SAUNA & HEALTH CLUB ☆☆☆
865, High Rd., Tottenham, N17 Ratings:A-6.B- .C-7.D-6.
Open 11-11. Tel. 880 9036 Basic Cost £10
Appearance: Staff young, racially varied & versatile, inc. ladies from Spain & Canada.
Car Parking: Park in front or at rear by Sainsbury's.
Ladies: 2 from 10 different Facilities: Sauna.

AFFINITY ☆☆☆
18E, High Rd., Willesden, NW10 Ratings:A-6.B- .C-4.D-7.
Open Mon-Fri 11.30-10.Sat-Sun 11.30-8. Tel. 459 0253. Basic Cost £16 A/V/AE
Appearance: Staff racially varied, young, slim & friendly, including ladies from Australia & Spain.
Car Parking: Park around the corner in Park Ave.
Ladies: 2 from 7 different. Facilities: Sunbeds & Steam Room.

ANGELS SAUNA ☆☆☆☆
371-373, Green St., Upton Park, E13. Ratings:A-7.B- .C-7.D-6.
Open 11- 10.30 Tel.470 9636 Basic Cost £10
Appearance: Staff all ages, shapes & sizes, versatile, racially varied & attractive.
Car Parking: Park around the corner in King's Rd.
Ladies: 2 from 14 different. Facilities: Sauna, Steam Room, Plunge pool & Sunbeds.

ANITAS ☆☆☆
463, High Rd., Leyton, E10. Ratings:A-7.B- .C-7.D-6.
Open 11-11. Tel.556 3345 Basic Cost £12
Appearance: Staff racially varied, young, all sizes & very versatile.
Car Parking: Before 7 park outside or opposite. After 7 use a side street.
Ladies: 2 from 10 different. Facilities: Sauna & Jacuzzi.

BAKERS ARMS SAUNA ☆☆☆
630A, Lea Bridge Rd., E10 Ratings:A-5.B- .C-4.D-5.
Open 11-11. Tel.518 7770 Basic Cost £12
Appearance: Staff cheerful & racially varied, but neither young nor slim.
Car Parking: Ideally park across the road, otherwise use Belmont Park Rd.
Ladies: 2 from 7 different. Facilities: Sauna.

BAY SAUNA ☆☆☆
25A, Lordship Lane, Tottenham, N17. Ratings:A-6.B- .C-7.D-6.
Open 12-12. Tel.365 1655 Basic Cost £10
Appearance: Staff youngish, slim & not unattractive. One from Brazil.
Car Parking: Park around the corner in Newlyn or Birkbeck Rd.
Ladies: 2 from 12 different. Facilities: Sauna & Air-bath.

CHINGFORD SAUNA & SOLARIA ☆☆☆
8, Hall Lane, Chingford, E4 Ratings:A-6.B- .C-5.D-6.
Open Mon-Fri 11-11.Sat-Sun 11-9. Tel. 524 0017. Basic Cost £11.
Appearance: Staff white, youngish & presentable.
Car Parking: Park over in Chingford mount shopper's car park or in Tufton Rd.
Ladies: 2 from 10 different. Facilities: Sauna & Jacuzzi.

COLINDALE SAUNA ☆☆☆
291, Edgware Rd., NW9 Ratings:A-7.B- .C-8.D-6.
Open 11-11 Tel 205 8850 Basic Cost £15
Appearance: Staff young, slim, friendly & not unattractive. One Chinese.
Car Parking: Park outside or opposite.
Ladies: 1 or 2 from 12 different. Facilities: Sauna

COSMO'S ☆☆☆
328, High Rd., Leyton, E10 Ratings:A-6.B- .C-6.D-6.
Open 11-10.30 Tel. 558 8918 Basic Cost £10
Appearance: Staff racially varied, young & slim inc. Chinese, Hawaiian & Filipino
Car Parking: Park around the corner in Tyndall Rd.
Ladies: 2 from 12 different. Facilities: Sauna

ELITE HARRINGAY SAUNA ☆☆☆
361, Green Lanes, Harringay, N4 Ratings:A-6.B- .C-7.D-6.
Open Mon-Sat 11-10.Sun 11.30-8. Tel.880 1434. Basic Cost £10
Appearance: Staff friendly, racially varied and mature. One Italian.
Car Parking: Park around the corner in Lothair Rd. North.
Ladies: 2 from 6 different. Facilities: Sauna

FANTASY SAUNA ☆☆☆☆
291, Archway Rd., Highgate, N6. Ratings:A-7.B- .C-4.D-5.
Open 11-1.30 Tel.347 9177 Basic Cost £15 A/V/AE/DC
Appearance: Staff young, racially varied, friendly & attractive.
Car Parking: Park around the corner in Jackson's Lane or Shepherds Hill.
Ladies: 2 from 10 different. Facilities: Sauna, Videos, Bubble Bath, Solarium & Gym.

GROVE SAUNA ☆☆☆
1127A, London Rd., SW16 Ratings:A-6.B- .C-7.D-6.
Open Mon-Fri 11-10.Sat-Sun 11-8. Tel.679 2252 Basic Cost £10.
Appearance: Staff young, versatile, racially varied & presentable.
Car Parking: Park in Pollards Hill South where access is.
Ladies:1 or 2 from 5 different. Facilities: Sauna, Plunge Pool & Fantasy Room.

HIGHAMS PARK SAUNA ☆☆☆☆
29A,Winchester Rd., Highams Park, E4. Ratings A-6.B- .C-8.D-7.
Open 11.30 - 9 Tel.531 1252 Basic Cost £15
Appearance: Staff versatile & all shapes, sizes & ages, inc. Polish, Thai, Italian & American ladies.
Car Parking: Park outside on pavement. Access through passageway at left.
Ladies: 2 from 14 different. Facilities: Sauna & Sunbed.

ISHKA BATH ☆☆☆
8, Hampden Rd., Hornsey, N8 Ratings A-7.B- .C-6.D-6.
Open Mon-Sat 12-10 Tel. 340 0973 Basic Cost £10
Appearance: Staff young, slim & mainly foreign, inc. Thai, Malaysian & Austrian ladies
Car Parking: Park around the corner in Wightman Rd.
Ladies: 3 from 15 different. Facilities: Bubble Bath.

LANACOMBE SAUNA ☆☆☆☆☆
70, Crouch End Hill, N8 Ratings A-8.B- .C-6.D-5.
Open:Mon-Sat 11-12.Sun 2-12. Tel.340 4677 Basic Cost £10
Appearance: Staff young, attractive, slim & shapely with ladies from Thailand, France, Germany, Poland, Russia & Brazil.
Car Parking: Park around the corner in Crescent Rd.
Ladies:8 to 11 from 36 different Facilities: Bubble Bath.

LEA BRIDGE SAUNA ☆☆
171,Lea Bridge Rd.,E10 Ratings A-5.B- .C-6.D-5.
Open:12-10 Tel.558 4585 Basic Cost £10
Appearance: Staff young, cheerful, racially varied & versatile.
Car Parking: Park across the road in Elm Park Rd.
Ladies:2 from 12 different. Facilities: Sauna.

NEW CITY SAUNA ☆☆☆
4, Grove Rd., Bow, E3 Ratings:A-6.B- .C-6.D-7
Open:11-11 Tel.983 7088 Basic Cost £10
Appearance: Staff youngish, all shapes, sizes & races, inc. one from Norway
Car Parking: Park outside or down the road.
Ladies:2 from 10 different. Facilities: Sauna, Sunbed & Videos.

NEW ELITE SAUNA ☆☆☆
27,Leytonstone Rd.,E15 Ratings A-6.B- .C-4.D-6.
Open: Mon-Sat 12-12 Tel. 221 0707 Basic Cost £10
Appearance: Staff all shapes, sizes, ages & races inc. Thai, Swedish & Spanish ladies.
Car Parking: Park around the corner in Francis St.
Ladies: 2 or 3 from 10 different Facilities: Sauna

PARADISE SAUNA & MASSAGE ☆☆☆☆
352, Neasden Lane, NW10 Ratings A-7.B- .C-5.D-5.
Open:11-12 Tel.208 1601 Basic Cost £15 A/V/AE/DC
Appearance: Staff white, versatile & young.
Car Parking: Just inside North Circular. Park in Neasden shopping centre.
Ladies: 2 from 10 different. Facilities: Sauna & Bubble Bath

PARK SAUNA
769, Romford Rd., Manor Park, E12 Ratings A- .B- .C-6.D- .
Open: Mon-Sat 11-11.Sun 11.30-10. Tel.553 0742 Basic Cost £10
Appearance: Money required up front. Would only say staff were white & versatile.
Car Parking: Park across the road in Meanley Rd. or First Ave.
Ladies: 2 from 8 different Facilities: Sauna

RUMORS ☆☆☆☆
85, Burdett Rd., Bow, E3 Ratings A-7.B- .C-8.D-7.
Open:11-1 Tel.983 4826 Basic Cost £15 A/V/AE/DC
Appearance: Staff youngish, versatile & white. One from Singapore, one French.
Car Parking: Park outside or in private car park.
Ladies: 2 from 10 different. Facilities: Sauna, Jacuzzi, Solarium & Gym.

SOLITAIRE ☆☆☆☆☆
2,Chatsworth Rd., Clapton, E5 Ratings A-8.B- .C-8.D-7.
Open: 4-4 Tel.985 0838 Basic Cost £10
Appearance: Staff young, slim & attractive, including several Thai ladies.
Car Parking: Park outside
Ladies:6 or 7 from 25 different. Facilities: Sauna, Jacuzzi, Steam Room & Sky T.V.

SPARKLES HEALTH CLUB ☆☆☆☆
66-68, Knights Hill, SE27 Ratings A-7.B- .C-5.D-6.
Open: Sun-Thurs 11-2.Fri-Sat 11-3. Tel. 761 0745. Basic Cost £5
Appearance: Staff young, shapely, racially varied, versatile & friendly.
Car Parking: Park around the corner in Wolfington Rd.
Ladies: 4 from 12 different Facilities: Videos

STERLING SAUNA ☆☆☆
42, Sterling Way, Edmonton, N18. Ratings A-5.B- .C-7.D-5.
Open: Mon-Sat 11-10.Sun 12-8 Tel. 807 8484 Basic Cost £10
Appearance: Staff slim & of varied age & race.
Car Parking: Park around the corner in College Close.
Ladies: 2 from 12 different. Facilities: Sauna

STRATFORD SAUNA ☆☆☆☆☆
164, The Grove, Stratford, E15 Ratings A-8.B- .C-7.D-7.
Open: Mon-Sat 12-2.Sun 3-12. Tel.555 7966. Basic Cost £10
Appearance: Friendly racially varied staff of all shapes & sizes including ladies from Thailand, China & the Philippines.
Car Parking: Park around the corner in Grove Crescent Rd.
Ladies: 5 from 20 different. Facilities: Sauna & Bubble Bath.

STREATHAM SAUNA ☆☆☆☆
Rear of 292, Streatham High Rd., SW16. Ratings A-7.B- .C-5.D-7.
Open: Mon-Sat 11-11.Sun 12-11. Tel.677 3615. Basic Cost £15 A/V
Appearance: Staff young, racially varied, attractive & all shapes & sizes.
Car Parking: Park nearby. Access from Babington Rd.
Ladies: 2 from 12 different. Facilities: Sauna, Jacuzzi, Gym & Sunbeds.

THAI SAUNA ☆☆☆☆
262, Langham Rd.,N15 Ratings: A-7.B- .C-5.D-5.
Open Mon-Sat 11-10.45.Sun 2-10.45. Tel.888 7667. Basic Cost £10
Appearance: Staff English, Irish or Asian, including ladies from Thailand, India & China, generally young & slim.
Tube Station: Use Turnpike Lane
Ladies: 5 from 20 different. Facilities: Bubble Bath

UTOPIA SAUNA ☆☆☆
825, Romford Rd., Manor Park, E12 Ratings A-5.B- .C-7.D-5.
Open 11-9.30. Tel. 514 5355 Basic Cost £10
Appearance: Staff white, friendly & all ages & sizes.
Car Parking: Park around the corner in Carlyle Rd.
Ladies:2 from 12 different. Facilities: Sauna

WANSTEAD SAUNA CLUB ☆☆☆
3c,High St.,Wanstead, E11 Ratings A-6.B- .C-8.D-6.
Open Mon-Sat 11-11.Sun 11-10. Tel. 989 4947. Basic Cost £10
Appearance: Staff white, friendly, versatile & all shapes, ages & sizes.
Car Parking: Park outside
Ladies: 2 from 10 different. Facilities: Sauna & Fantasy Room

WILLESDEN SAUNA ☆☆☆☆
140, High Rd., Willesden, NW10. Ratings A-7.B- .C-4.D-6.
Open 12-12 Tel.830 2008/2855 Basic Cost £15
Appearance: Staff versatile, slim & racially varied including ladies from France, Italy and Greece.
Car Parking: Park around the corner in Gowan or Sandringham Rd.
Ladies: 2 from 7 different. Facilities: Sauna

SIDCUP- 0181

BODYMATTERS ☆☆☆
242A, Blackfen Rd. Ratings A-5.B- .C-7.D-6.
Open 11.30-9.30 Tel. 294 1950 Basic Cost £10
Appearance: Staff white, versatile & all ages - one Italian.
Car Parking: Park on pavement in front of neighbouring Kor-Kies Fashions
Ladies:2 from 10 different Facilities: Sauna

WELLING - 0181

WELLING MASSAGE ☆☆
65, High St. Ratings: A-4.B- .C-3.D-6.
Open 11-9 Tel.304 2965 Basic Cost: £10
Appearance: Staff all ages, white & versatile.
Car Parking: Park down Danson Lane opposite.
Ladies:1 from 5 different Facilities:

WEMBLEY - 0181

WEMBLEY SAUNA ☆☆☆☆
4, The Broadway, Preston Rd. Ratings: A-7.B- .C-7.D-6.
Open 11-12. Tel.904 0393 Basic Cost £15
Appearance: Staff young, slim & generally attractive, including one lady who is half-Spanish and half-Egyptian.
Car Parking: Park around the corner in Preston Rd.
Ladies: 3 from 12 different. Facilities: Sauna

GREATER MANCHESTER

Greater Manchester comprises a number of different boroughs but massage is only licensed in some of them. So while Greater Manchester must be regarded as the massage capital of the country with over 50 parlours liberally dotted around the county, in certain areas there are none - to be precise - there are none in Stockport, Bolton, Tameside or Rochdale. However in Manchester, Salford, Trafford, Bury & Oldham there are many parlours, plus a couple in the Leigh area of the Wigan metropolitan district.

When it comes to massage Manchester does indeed boast both the best & the worst that this country can offer. In Burnage, a quiet district straddling the main A34 in the south-east of the city is Hayley's - simply the parlour with the most attractive women in the whole country. When they say the ladies working there are beautiful - they mean it. Indeed the vast majority of them would not look out of place in a Miss World pageant. The first time I went to look over the establishment - it is located discreetly tucked away over a pizza parlour - I would have been welcome to take my turn to see the ladies but I would have had to have waited behind 4 other men awaiting their massage in turn. The same happened the second time I visited the place. On my third visit I waited & was treated to a view of, quite simply, Heaven on Earth. And as you wait you are taken care of - given a drink, a choice of papers to read, Everton mints to suck & the television to watch. On my fourth visit, I arrived soon after opening hours & was soon introduced to both the ladies available - both potential Miss World candidates. And I have been independently told the quality of the massage is just as good.

Manchester Central / West

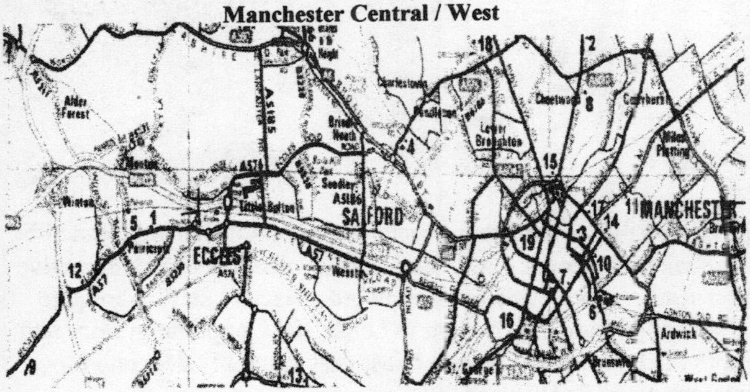

1 Adam & Eve
2 Apollo
3 Birds of Paradise
4 Boardrooms
5 Chelsea's
6 Chesterfield's
7 Cosmopolitan
8 Destiny
9 The Gallery
10 Maralena's
11 New Casbah
12 New Silver Lady
13 Park Avenue
14 Piccadilly
15 Salon 24
16 Sheer Delight
17 Shelley's
18 Stephanie's
19 Xanadu

And when it comes to facilities Manchester again boasts the best. At Chesterfields in Whitworth St. the facilities available are second to none - a fully equipped gymnasium, large screen Sky T.V. in a luxury lounge, a steam room & sauna and in each massage room a generous sized jacuzzi plus whirlpool baths.

But to be fair, Manchester excels at the other end of the spectrum as well. In Hyde Rd. are some of the least attractive parlours I have seen in the entire country. And I would not get excited about Shelley's, Number 17, Lady Jane Health Studio, New Casbah or Birds of Paradise.

Excellence is not just to be found at Hayley's & Chesterfields. Dotted around the city are a fair number of first class establishments. One group all under the same management comprises Chelsea's, Stephanie's & Vanessa's; all are pretty basic establishments so far as facilities are concerned, though the decor, particularly at Stephanie's is superb. And I must add they have an engagingly attractive range of masseuses. In Oldham & Cadishead are the Georgian & the Gallery, again under the same management. Here you find not only first class looking staff, with an interesting smattering of exotic foreign ladies working but decent sized beds in pleasantly decorated rooms, the V.I.P. suite at the Gallery being particularly well appointed.

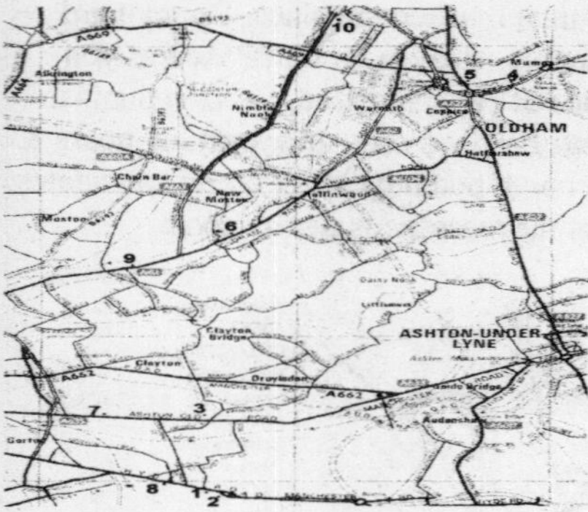

Manchester East

1 Aphrodite's
2 Club 826
3 Connections
4 The Georgian
5 Jackson's
6 Lady Jane Health Studio
7 Mystique
8 New Honey's
9 Samantha's
10 Silks

Right
A luxury massage room at The Georgian

Out on the fringe of the city are a number of interesting establishments. Radcliffe, near Bury boasts two - Dreams & Gemini - both are tastefully decorated with attractive looking bunches of ladies.Rather more basic but again with attractive staff, who quite obviously want to take care of you are the Lyceum in Leigh, the Lamplight in Bury and Louisa's in Walkden. Both the Lyceum & Louisa's boast very tastefully decorated waiting areas where one can easily feel relaxed.

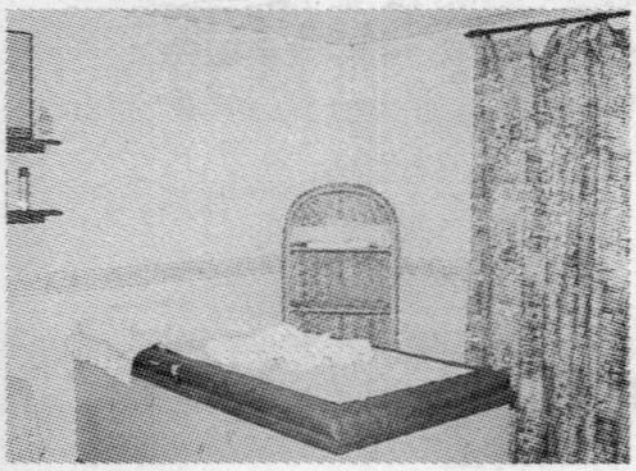

Left
A massage room at Louisa's

Right
The V.I.P. room at Gemini

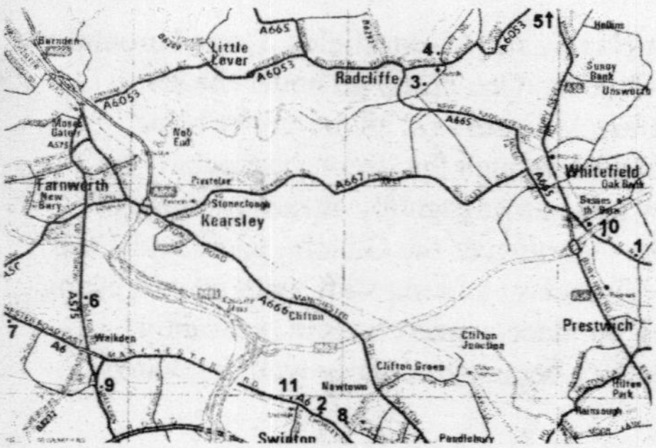

Manchester North

1 Coco's
2 Cupid's
3 Dreams
4 Gemini
5 The Lamplight
6 Louisa's
7 Nicole's
8 Number 17
9 Polly's
10 Tiffany's
11 Toucan Club

Tiffany's in Whitefield, while only a basic parlour, does boast an attractive selection of ladies, able to cater to your every whim.

Out in Oldham, as well as The Georgian, the town boasts Jackson's, a small inexpensive establishment, pleasantly decorated with attractive staff and a friendly receptionist.

Just south of the city centre are four more parlours, where the people running them want to do their best for their clientele. Park Avenue on the Trafford Park industrial estate has a range of attractive ladies working with first class facilities. At Penelope's in West Didsbury, there is a somewhat international flavour to the staff with ladies from Spain & the Philippines. At Devines in Slade Lane, Levenshulme besides attractive young staff they boast a reasonably equipped fantasy room. Last but not least, although Pandora's in Wilmslow Rd. is pretty basic, they are open almost 24 hours a day and also boast attractive staff, unlike many of the other 24 hours a day establishments.

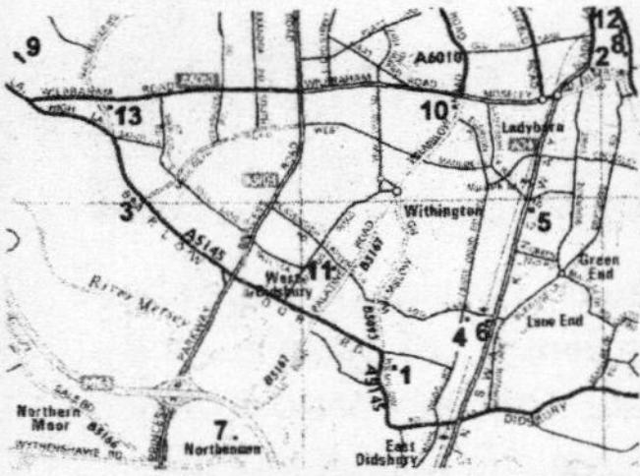

Manchester South
1 Charlotte's
2 Devine's
3 Director's Lodge
4 Galaxy
5 Hayley's Health Studio
6 Kingsway Health Club
7 Ladybirds
8 Marie's
9 Moulin Rouge
10 Pandora's
11 Penelope's
12 Sunflower
13 Vanessa's

The waiting lounge at Director's Lodge

Also on the south side of the city is a newly opened establishment located over a charity shop - under the same management as Kellie's in Warrington - The Director's Lodge has an impressive waiting room as well as delightful looking staff. The south side of the city also has two more parlours of note. Ladybirds in Northenden is one of the few parlours in Manchester where they obviously feel the heat. The ladies are uniformly dressed in their underwear. Kingsway Health Club, located over a car showroom in Burnage has extensive facilities and not bad looking ladies in attendance.

Left
Salon 24

Right
The Fantasy room at Salon 24

In the Manchester city centre are two more gems - Salon 24 and Xanadu. At Salon 24 besides the most enormous massage bench I have ever seen the establishment boasts secure parking, attractive staff, videos and a fantasy room with a first class range of equipment.

Xanadu, with limited on site parking at the rear of the premises, besides the normal massage available, also boasts a mixed sauna club. This operates most evenings for couples or individuals who wish to meet up with like minded people. Tuesday evenings and Sunday lunchtimes are given over to strippers, while the facilities also

Xanadu
Left
The waiting lounge

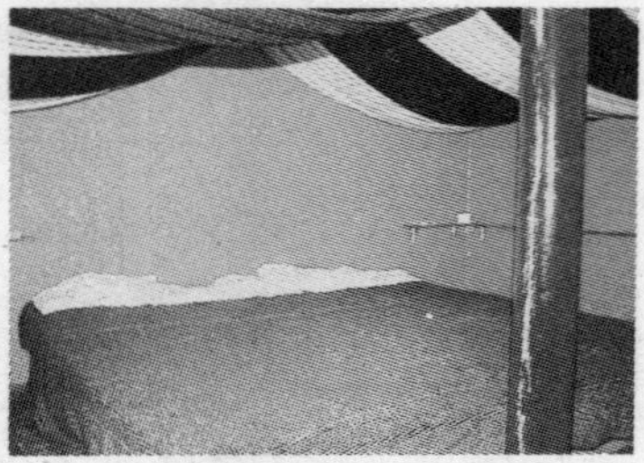

Right
The bedroom for like minded people

stretch to a voyeur's suite and a giant bed for group sessions. To partake in the above you need to formally join the Xanadu adult club. If one is thinking of doing so, one should bear in mind that you need to be pretty unshockable. One lady parlour owner from elsewhere in the country told me that having visited Xanadu to look into the possibility of opening her parlour to mixed sauna evenings, she had not thought she would be shocked but she was there.

Also in the city centre in Cosmopolitan. I have been independently informed this is one of the best parlours in the city, but I was not so impressed when I visited it, maybe I caught them on an off day. I intend to check the place out again before producing the next guide. There are a fair number of other parlours close to the city centre but few of the others impressed me, though Piccadilly does have an interesting international range of ladies working there.

BURY - 0161

The LAMPLIGHT ☆☆☆☆
27, Bolton Rd. Ratings A-7.B- .C-6.D-5.
Open 11- 9 Tel. 763 5224 Basic Cost
Appearance: Staff youngish, white, versatile & not unattractive.
Car Parking: Difficult - suggest along the road outside Blockbusters.
Ladies: 1 from 7 different. Facilities: Videos.

LEIGH - 01942

LEIGH SAUNA ☆
135, Chapel St. Ratings A-3.B- .C-8.D-5.
Open Mon-Fri 11-9.Sat 11-5. Tel. 602987 Basic Cost £10.
Appearance: Staff mature but versatile.
Car Parking: Park around the corner in Lingard St.
Ladies: 2 from 3 different. Facilities: Sauna

The LYCEUM ☆☆☆☆
38, St. Helen's Rd. Ratings A-7.B- .C-8.D-6.
Open Mon-Sat 11-9. Sun 11-8. Tel. 670300 Basic Cost
Appearance: Staff youngish, racially varied & attractive.
Car Parking: Park at back of car radio shop. Entrance at rear.
Ladies: 1 or 2 from 10 different. Facilities: Sauna, Jacuzzi & Sunbeds.

MANCHESTER - 0161

ADAM & EVE
206, Liverpool Rd., Eccles Ratings A- .B- .C-7.D- .
Open 11-8 (Mixed Sauna Club after 8) Tel. 789 8500 Basic Cost
Appearance: Money required up front.
Car Parking: Park across the road in Bradburn Close.
Ladies: 1 different each week. Facilities: Sauna & Videos.

APHRODITE'S ☆☆
782A, Hyde Rd. Ratings A-4.B- .C-8.D-5.
Open 11.30 - 10. Tel. 231 7201 Basic Cost £10
Appearance: Staff white, youngish & versatile.
Car Parking: Park around the corner in Friendship Ave.
Ladies: 2 from 8 different. Facilities: Videos.

APOLLO ☆☆☆
480, Cheetham Hill Rd. Ratings A-5.B-6.C-6.D-5.
Open 10-10 Tel. 795 4944 Basic Cost
Appearance: Staff white, versatile, all ages & sizes.
Car Parking: Park across the road in Grangeforth Rd.
Ladies: 2 from 10 different. Facilities: Videos.

BIRDS OF PARADISE ☆☆
1A, Kelvin St. Ratings A-3.B- .C-3.D-6.
Open 10-10 Tel. 834 7440 Basic Cost
Appearance: Staff young, racially varied & versatile.
Car Parking: Parking awkward. Meters available here & there.
Ladies: 2 from 10 different. Facilities: Videos.

CHARLOTTE'S ☆☆☆
743A, Wilmslow Rd. Ratings A-6.B- .C-6.D-5.
Open 11-9. Tel. 434 0135 Basic Cost £10.
Appearance: Staff youngish, versatile & all shapes & sizes. One Half-Maltese.
Car Parking: Park around the corner in Elm Grove.
Ladies: 2 from 10 different. Facilities: Sauna

CHELSEA'S ☆☆☆☆
232, Liverpool Rd., Eccles Ratings A-7.B- .C-7.D-6.
Open 11-9. Tel.707 1862 Basic Cost
Appearance: Staff young & versatile, inc. French, Spanish, Thai & Mexican ladies.
Car Parking: Park around the corner in Shakespeare Cres.
Ladies: 2 from 15 different. Facilities:

CHESTERFIELDS ☆☆☆☆☆
6, Whitworth St. Ratings A-8.B- .C-4.D-9.
Open 11-9.30 Tel. 237 3899 Basic Cost £15 A/V
Appearance: Staff young, racially varied & attractive. One Filipino.
Car Parking: Find a pay & display or meter nearby.
Ladies: 2 from 10 different. Facilities: Sauna, Jacuzzis, Steam Room, Gymnasium & Sky TV

CLUB 826 ☆☆
826, Hyde Rd. Ratings A-5.B- .C-7.D-5.
Open 24 hours a day - 7 days a week. Tel. 230 7927 Basic Cost £5
Appearance: Staff young, racially varied & versatile.
Car Parking: Park around the corner in Woodland Rd.
Ladies: 2 from 12 different. Facilities: Videos & Herbal Bath.

COCO'S ☆☆☆
464, Bury Old Rd., Prestwich Ratings A-5.B- .C-8.D-4.
Open 11- 8.30 Tel. 773 5030 Basic Cost
Appearance: Staff all ages, racially varied & versatile. One Thai.
Car Parking: Park in front.
Ladies: 2 from 12 different. Facilities: Videos.

CONNECTIONS ☆☆☆
141, Old Lane, Openshaw Ratings A-6.B- .C-8.D-6.
Open 11-8. Tel. 301 2011 Basic Cost A/V.
Appearance: Staff mainly more mature, white & very versatile.
Car Parking: Park in front.
Ladies: 2 from 10 different. Facilities: Jacuzzi, Videos & Fantasy Room.

COSMOPOLITAN ☆☆☆☆
44, Portland St. Ratings:A-7.B- .C-2.D-5.
Open 11-4. Tel.236 6307 Basic Cost £8
Appearance: Staff white, all ages, shapes & sizes.
Car Parking: Difficult to park in city centre. Find a meter nearby.
Ladies: 2 from 16 different. Facilities: Sauna

CUPIDS ☆☆☆
Corner of Sutherland & Rutland St., Swinton Ratings:A-5.B- .C-7.D-8.
Open 11-8. Tel. 794 8877 Basic Cost
Appearance: Staff white, youngish & versatile. One half-Spanish
Car Parking: Park across the road in Rutland St.
Ladies: 2 or 3 from 14 different. Facilities: Videos, Pool table & Large Screen TV.

DESTINY ☆☆☆
182, Stocks St., Cheetham Ratings:A-7.B- .C-8.D-6.
Open Mon-Fri 12-10.Sat-Sun 11-8.30. Tel.833 2511 Basic Cost.
Appearance: Staff youngish, versatile & not unattractive. One from Brazil.
Car Parking: Located at very top of street. Park opposite.
Ladies: 2 from 10 different. Facilities:

DEVINES ☆☆☆☆
322, Slade Lane, Levenshulme Ratings:A-7.B- .C-7.D-6.
Open Mon-Fri 11-10.Sat 11-2. Tel. 225 2793. Basic Cost
Appearance: Staff racially varied, very versatile & all ages and sizes.
Car Parking: Park outside or opposite.
Ladies: 2 from 6 different. Facilities: Sauna, Videos & Fantasy Room.

DIRECTOR'S LODGE ☆☆☆☆☆
365A, Barlow Moor Rd. Ratings:A-8.B- .C-9.D-8.
Open 11-9 Tel. 861 7199 Basic Cost £10 A/V
Appearance: Staff young, racially varied & versatile, inc. Spanish & Swedish ladies.
Car Parking: Park in front. Entrance at side.
Ladies: 2 from 10 different. Facilities: Jacuzzi & Video.

DREAMS ☆☆☆☆
55, Church St., Radcliffe Ratings:A-7.B-4.C-8.D-7.
Open Mon-Fri 11-9.Sat 11-8.30.Sun 12-8.30 Tel.725 8295 Basic Cost A/V
Appearance: Staff youngish, versatile, racially varied & all shapes & sizes.
Car Parking: Park in free public car park at rear.
Ladies: 2 from 13 different. Facilities: Sauna, Jacuzzi, Videos & Jungle room.

GALAXY ☆☆
2, Elmsmere Rd., Didsbury Ratings:A-4.B- .C-9.D-5.
Open 11-10. Tel.445 2207. Basic Cost £10.
Appearance: Staff racially varied, mature & versatile.
Car Parking: Park in road in front.
Ladies: 2 from 10 different. Facilities: Sauna.

The GALLERY ☆☆☆☆☆
199, Liverpool Rd., Cadishead Ratings:A-8.B- .C-8.D-8.
Open 11-10.30 Tel.777 6745 Basic Cost £10 A/V/AE.
Appearance: Staff racially varied, young & attractive inc. a Russian & a page 3 lady.
Car Parking: Park around the corner in Green Lane, where entrance is.
Ladies: 3 from 20 different. Facilities: Videos & Jacuzzis.

GEMINI ☆☆☆☆☆
13, Bury Rd., Radcliffe Ratings:A-7.B-7.C-7.D-6.
Open 11-8.30 Tel.723 5430 Basic Cost A/V
Appearance: Staff young, white, versatile & attractive. One lady is French.
Car Parking: Park across the road in Schofield St.
Ladies: 2 from 12 different. Facilities: Sauna, Jacuzzis, Videos, Sky TV & Uniforms.

HAYLEY'S HEALTH STUDIO ☆☆☆☆☆
269A, Kingsway, Burnage Ratings:A-9.B-7.C-6.D-8.
Open 10.30-9. Tel. 432 3732 Basic Cost £10
Appearance: Staff white, young, versatile & very attractive including one lady who is half Swedish - half Irish.
Car Parking: Park in front or around the corner in Broadhill Rd.
Ladies: 2 from 10 different. Facilities: Sauna

KINGSWAY HEALTH CLUB ☆☆☆☆
370, Kingsway, Burnage Ratings:A-6.B- .C-7.D-6.
Open 11-10. Tel. 432 3957 Basic Cost
Appearance: Staff youngish, racially varied & versatile.
Car Parking: Park in Fog Lane. Premises over car showrooms.
Ladies: 2 from 10 different. Facilities: Sauna, Jacuzzi, Gym & Solarium.

LADY JANE HEALTH STUDIO ☆
348, Oldham Rd., Failsworth Ratings: A-3.B- .C-7.D-3.
Open 11-9. Tel. 683 5578 Basic Cost
Appearance: Staff white, versatile and all ages, shapes & sizes.
Car Parking: Park around the corner in Valentine St.
Ladies: 2 from 6 different. Facilities: Videos & Fantasy Room.

LADYBIRDS ☆☆☆☆
309B, Palatine Rd., Northenden Ratings: A-7.B- .C-5.D-6.
Open 11-10. Tel. 945 1962. Basic Cost
Appearance: Staff young, racially varied, versatile & scantily attired.
Car Parking: Park around the corner in Allanson Rd.
Ladies: 2 from 12 different. Facilities:

LOUISA'S ☆☆☆☆
2B, Louisa St., Walkden Ratings: A-7.B- .C-6.D-7.
Open 11.30 - 8.30 Tel.703 7077 Basic Cost £5
Appearance: Staff white, versatile and attractive. One is American. One is a Qualified Aromatherapist.
Car Parking: Park around the corner in Harriet St.
Ladies: 2 from 7 different. Facilities: Sunbed & Videos.

MARALENA'S ☆☆☆
15, Paton St., Piccadilly Ratings: A-6.B- .C-3.D-6.
Open Mon-Fri 11.30 -5. Tel. 236 7069 Basic Cost
Appearance: Staff white, cheerful, cuddly & friendly.
Car Parking: Park on a meter nearby if you can.
Ladies: 1 lady. Facilities: Sunbed

MARIE'S ☆☆☆
906A, Stockport Rd., Levenshulme. Ratings: A-5.B- .C-7.D-5.
Open 11-10. Tel. 248 9363 Basic Cost £7
Appearance: Staff white, young & very versatile.
Car Parking: Park in Farm Side Place where entrance is.
Ladies 2 from 6 different. Facilities: Videos

MOULIN ROUGE ☆☆
4A, Longford Rd., Stretford. Ratings:A-6.B- .C-7.D-4.
Open 12-10. Tel. 866 8896 Basic Cost £7
Appearance: Staff versatile & generally young. One Asian.
Car Parking: Park on the road in front.
Ladies: 1 from 7 different. Facilities: Videos.

MYSTIQUE ☆☆☆
819A, Ashton Old Rd. Ratings:A-6.B- .C-7.D-4.
Open 11-9. Tel.223 5512 Basic Cost
Appearance: Staff white, young and versatile.
Car Parking: Park around the corner in Wood St.
Ladies: 2 from 9 different. Facilities: Jacuzzi, Fantasy Room & Videos.

NEW CASBAH ☆☆
128, Oldham Rd. Ratings:A-5.B- .C-8.D-5.
Open 24 hours a day - 7 days a week Tel. 205 5044 Basic Cost £10.
Appearance: Staff white, young & versatile.
Car Parking: Park around the back in Portugal St., off Radium St.
Ladies: 2 from 10 different. Facilities: Videos.

NEW HONEY'S ☆☆
638A, Hyde Rd., Gorton Ratings: A-4.B-4.C-8.D-5.
Open 24 hours a day - 7 days a week. Tel. 223 3051. Basic Cost £5
Appearance: Staff white, young & versatile.
Car Parking: Park around the corner in Peacock Grove.
Ladies: 2 from 10 different. Facilities: Videos & Fantasy Room.

NEW SILVER LADY ☆☆
628, Liverpool Rd., Eccles Ratings: A-4.B- .C-9.D-6.
Open Mon-Sat 11-8 Tel. 707 0800 Basic Cost £10
Appearance: Staff mature, versatile and all shapes & sizes
Car Parking: Park at rear of premises off Gorton Rd.
Ladies: 2 from 6 different Facilities: Sauna

NICOLE'S ☆☆☆
177A, Manchester Rd. East, Walkden. Ratings:A-6.B- .C-8.D-5.
Open 11-9 Tel. 703 8220 Basic Cost
Appearance: Staff young, versatile, white & attractive.
Car Parking: Over motor spare parts shop. Park on land at side.
Ladies: 1 from 5 different. Facilities: Sauna

NUMBER 17 ☆☆☆
17, Station Rd., Swinton Ratings:A-4.B- .C-6.D-5.
Open Mon-Sat 11-8.30 Tel. 794 9386 Basic Cost
Appearance: Staff white, versatile & generally relatively mature.
Car Parking: Park in shopping centre car park in Chadwick St.
Ladies: 1 from 7 different. Facilities: Videos.

PANDORA'S ☆☆☆☆
310, Wilmslow Rd., Fallowfield Ratings:A-7.B- .C-7.D-5.
Open 24 hours a day,7 days a week Tel.248 8808 Basic Cost
Appearance: Staff young, attractive & versatile, including ladies from Russia, Sweden & Brazil.
Car Parking: Park in front or around the corner in Wynnstay Grove.
Ladies: 2 from 30 different. Facilities: Sauna & Videos.

PARK AVENUE ☆☆☆☆
3A, Third Ave., Trafford Park Ratings:A-7.B- .C-7.D-5.
Open Mon-Sat 10-10. Sun 10.30 -10. Tel.876 6033 Basic Cost
Appearance: Staff young, presentable, racially varied & versatile.
Car Parking: Park in the road outside.
Ladies: 2 from 7 different Facilities: Sauna & Videos.

PENELOPE'S ☆☆☆☆
40B, Lapwing Lane, West Didsbury. Ratings:A-7.B- .C-7.D-7.
Open: Mon-Sat 11-9.30.Sun 12-9.30. Tel.445 5958 Basic Cost £8
Appearance: Staff all ages & versatile, including one Spanish & one Filipino lady.
Car Parking: Park around the corner in Raleigh Close.
Ladies: 2 from 10 different. Facilities: Jacuzzi, Videos & Fantasy Room.

PICCADILLY ☆☆☆
38, Great Ancoats St. Ratings:A-6.B- .C-3.D-6.
Open:24 hours a day - 7 days a week Tel. 237 9291 Basic Cost
Appearance: Staff young & versatile inc. Spanish, Italian, Brazilian & Filipino ladies.
Car Parking: Try and find a meter somewhere nearby.
Ladies: 2 from 12 different. Facilities: Sauna & Videos.

POLLY'S ☆☆☆
152A, Walkden Rd., Walkden Ratings:A-5.B- .C-7.D-4.
Open 11-8. Tel.703 8139 Basic Cost £10
Appearance: Staff young, white, cheerful & versatile. One half-Italian.
Car Parking: Park around the corner in Royle St.
Ladies: 2 from 10 different. Facilities:

SALON 24 ☆☆☆☆☆
24, Park St. Ratings:A-7.B- .C-9.D-7.
Open 11-12. Tel. 839 6446 Basic Cost A/V/AE
Appearance: Staff youngish, white, very versatile & shapely.
Car Parking: Drive in through gates & park on premises.
Ladies: 2 from 7 different. Facilities: Videos & Fantasy Room.

SAMANTHA'S ☆☆☆
977, Oldham Rd., Newton Heath. Ratings:A-6.B- .C-6.D-5.
Open 11-8.30 Tel. 682 1206 Basic Cost £6
Appearance: Staff young, all shapes & sizes, white & versatile.
Car Parking: Park around the back having turned into Erwin St.
Ladies: 2 from 7 different. Facilities:

SHEER DELIGHT ☆☆☆
364A, Deansgate Ratings:A-6.B- .C-4.D-5.
Open 12-10 Tel. 832 7811 Basic Cost
Appearance: Staff young, white, versatile & moderately attractive.
Car Parking: Park around the corner in Whitworth St. West on a meter.
Ladies: 2 from 8 different. Facilities: Sauna, Jacuzzi, Videos & Fantasy Room.

SHELLEY'S ☆☆
24A, Swan St. Ratings: A-3.B- .C-4.D-3.
Open 11- 9.30 Tel.839 7062 Basic Cost
Appearance: Staff racially varied, versatile & cuddly.
Car Parking: Park around the corner in Cross Keys St.
Ladies: 2 from 10 different. Facilities: Videos & Fantasy Room.

SUNFLOWER ☆☆☆
892A, Stockport Rd., Levenshulme. Ratings:A-6.B- .C-8.D-6.
Open: Sun-Thurs 12-12.Fri-Sat 12-3. Tel. 257 3595 Basic Cost
Appearance: Staff young, shapely, versatile & racially varied.
Car Parking: Park in Carrill Grove where entrance is.
Ladies: 2 from 10 different. Facilities: Videos

TIFFANY'S ☆☆☆☆
74A, Bury Old Rd., Whitefield Ratings:A-7.B- .C-7.D-6.
Open: 11-9 Tel. 773 8608 Basic Cost
Appearance: Staff young, white, versatile & attractive.
Car Parking: Park around the corner in Walker Ave.
Ladies: 2 from 12 different. Facilities:

TOUCAN CLUB ☆☆☆
467A, Chorley Rd., Swinton Ratings:A-5.B- .C-6.D-5.
Open: 12-10 Tel. 794 6588 Basic Cost A/V
Appearance: Staff racially varied, versatile & all ages, shapes & sizes.
Car Parking: Park around the corner in Moss Lane
Ladies: 2 from 10 different. Facilities:Videos & Fantasy Rooms.

VANESSA'S ☆☆☆☆☆
430A, Barlow Moor Rd., Chorlton Ratings: A-8.B-8.C-5.D-7.
Open: 11-9. Tel. 861 7302 Basic Cost
Appearance: Staff young, friendly, versatile & attractive, including one lady from Peru.
Car Parking: Park opposite in Groby Rd.
Ladies: 2 from 12 different. Facilities:

XANADU ☆☆☆☆☆
14, Blackfriars St. Ratings: A-8.B- .C-8.D-7.
Open: 11-8. Tel. 839 9559 Basic Cost
Appearance: Staff young, racially varied & generally attractive.
Car Parking: Park around the back on premises off Booth St.
Ladies: 2 from 10 different. Facilities: Jacuzzi, Videos & Mixed Sauna Club.

OLDHAM - 0161

The GEORGIAN ☆☆☆☆☆
8, Waterloo St. Ratings: A-8.B-8 C-3.D-8.
Open: 10.30-10.30. Tel. 678 7916 Basic Cost £10 A/V
Appearance: Staff young, very versatile & attractive inc. ladies from Brazil & Australia.
Car Parking: Find a meter nearby.
Ladies: 3 from 10 different. Facilities: Jacuzzis, Videos & Stoneroom.

JACKSONS ☆☆☆☆
17, Jackson Pit Ratings: A-7.B- .C-5.D-7.
Open: 11-9. Tel. 626 6674 Basic Cost £5
Appearance: Staff white, versatile, presentable & all shapes, ages & sizes.
Car Parking: Park on a meter nearby or use Halfords.
Ladies: 1 from 3 different. Facilities: Videos.

SILKS ☆☆☆
90B, Broadway, Chadderton Ratings: A-5.B- .C-9.D-6.
Open 11-8.30 Tel. 633 1065 Basic Cost £10 A/V
Appearance: Staff white, versatile & all ages, shapes & sizes.
Car Parking: Turn into Burnley Lane & use free car park by entrance.
Ladies: 2 from 10 different. Facilities: Videos & Uniforms.

SALFORD - 0161

BOARDROOMS ☆☆
1, Cheltenham St. Ratings: A-4.B- C-7.D-5.
Open 11- 7.30 Tel. 736 5849 Basic Cost
Appearance: Staff young, versatile & all shapes & sizes. One Filipino.
Car Parking: Park outside or in free car park off Gloucester St
Ladies: 2 from 6 different. Facilities: Videos & Jacuzzi.

STEPHANIES ☆☆☆☆☆
340, Great Clowes St., Higher Broughton. Ratings: A-8.B- .C-9.D-7.
Open 11-9 Tel. 792 8606 Basic Cost
Appearance: Staff young, racially varied, attractive & versatile, including one lady from Spain.
Car Parking: Park in front.
Ladies: 2 from 12 different. Facilities: Jacuzzi

HAMPSHIRE

It is with disappointment that I find myself writing about Hampshire. Despite the presence of the two great cities of Portsmouth & Southampton, massage is ill catered for in this neck of the woods.

All I could find were three parlours & three disappointing ones at that. Although the staff working in them are apparently reasonably versatile, one would find far more in Hove or Bristol or many other places further north.

FAREHAM - 01329

HEATHER SCOTT ☆☆☆
30E, Catisfield Lane Ratings:A-5.B- .C-9.D-4.
Open Mon-Sat 10.30-8 Tel. 314151 Basic Cost: £30
Appearance: Lady is youngish, white, versatile & cheerful
Car Parking: Located in an unusual commercial unit. Park outside.
Ladies: One lady Facilities:

SOUTHAMPTON - 01703

BODYTOURS ☆☆☆
Basement Flat, Corner of New Rd. & Palmerston Rd. Ratings:A-5.B- .C-6.D-5.
Open Mon-Sat 11.30-9 Tel. 232718 Basic Cost £30
Appearance: Staff youngish, friendly, racially varied & versatile.
Car Parking: Park down Palmerston Rd. using pay & display.
Ladies: 1 from 6 different. Facilities:

UNIT TWO ☆☆
Unit 2, 78, Portswood Rd. Ratings:A-5.B- .C-8.D-6.
Open Mon-Sat 11-10. Tel. 583538 Basic Cost: £20
Appearance: Staff white, one in 20's.One in 30's.
Car Parking: Unit in office complex. Park outside.
Ladies: 1 from 2 different. Facilities:

HERTFORDSHIRE

Immediately to the north of Greater London lies Hertfordshire, where hurricanes hardly ever happen. Massage does however, particularly in that epitome of suburbia Watford. This town boasts five parlours, two of which are genuinely first class establishments - Bushey Sauna & Watford Health Studio. Both are basic establishments with only sauna facilities, but both have attractive staff.

Also in the top notch category is Palms in Ware, which has for some sessions, the most attractive ladies I have come across in the south-east, one of whom is quite prepared to serenade you while giving you a massage!!! Also unusually they have an Arabic masseuse.

Finally the last parlour of note is the Classic Club in Hemel Hempstead. This establishment also boasts a first class Stoneroom., indeed quite possibly the best one I have seen in the entire south-east with a complete range of equipment. It should be noted that, while under the same roof as the massage establishment it is only available by prior appointment for use with a lady who specialises in Fantasy sessions.

HEMEL HEMPSTEAD - 01442

CLASSIC CLUB ☆☆☆☆
85, The Marlowes Ratings:A-7.B- .C-6.D-7.
Open 11-10. Tel. 230013 Basic Cost £25
Appearance: Staff young, versatile & all shapes & sizes. One Thai.
Car Parking: Ideally park on premises obtaining window ticket to avoid clamping.
Ladies: 2 from 12 different. Facilities: Sauna, Jacuzzi, Videos & Stoneroom

WARE - 01920

PALMS ☆☆☆☆
116, High St. Ratings:A-7.B- .C-5.D-6.
Open Mon-Sat 11-8 Tel. 467434 Basic Cost £15
Appearance: Staff youngish, versatile & attractive. One Arabic.
Car Parking: Park in Priory St., off opposite side of road.
Ladies: 2 from 12 different. Facilities: Sauna.

WATFORD - 01923

BUSHEY SAUNA ☆☆☆☆
1, Chalk Hill, Bushey Ratings:A-7.B- .C-8.D-5.
Open 10.30-12 Tel. 219911 Basic Cost £15 A/V
Appearance: Staff young, white, attractive & all shapes & sizes.
Car Parking: Park in front or in neighbouring free car park.
Ladies: 2 from 10 different. Facilities: Sauna

A DIFFERENT SAUNA ☆☆☆
93, Market St. Ratings:A-6.B- .C-4.D-5.
Open Mon-Fri 11-9.30. Sat 12-9. Sun 1-8. Tel.213253. Basic Cost £15 A/V.
Appearance: Staff young, white, friendly & versatile, inc. ladies from Italy & Sweden.
Car Parking: Ideally park outside. Otherwise use Addiscombe Rd. or Fearnley St.
Ladies: 3 from 10 different. Facilities: Sauna

PAMPERS ☆☆
99, Vicarage Rd. Ratings:A-6.B- .C-6.D-4.
Open Mon-Sat 11.30-6. Tel. 211535 Basic Cost £12
Appearance: Staff racially varied, young & slimmish.
Car Parking: Park around the corner in Oxford St.
Ladies: 2 ladies. Facilities:

SUMMER HOUSE ☆☆☆
55, Market St. Ratings:A-5.B- .C-4.D-5.
Open Mon-Fri 12.30-10.30.Sat-Sun 1-8. Tel. 245112. Basic Cost £15.
Appearance: Staff mature, cheerful, friendly, racially varied & versatile, inc. an Italian.
Car Parking: Ideally park outside. Alternatively use Addiscombe Rd. or Fearnley St.
Ladies: 2 from 10 different. Facilities: Sauna

WATFORD HEALTH STUDIO ☆☆☆☆
33, Upton Rd. Ratings:A-7.B- .C-5.D-5.
Open: 11-9. Tel. 226017 Basic Cost £15
Appearance: Staff white, all ages, slim, versatile and presentable.
Car Parking: Park in front or in nearby Addiscombe or Whippendell Rd.
Ladies: 2 from 12 different. Facilities: Sauna

KENT

In the garden of England there are five parlours that I have been able to find and they make up an interesting selection. Three are in the Medway towns and although expensive compared to the establishments available up north still offer reasonable value for money.

Oasis Sauna and Massage in Chatham, though basically inexpensive, has some attractive ladies working there but they can be a little short with their prospective clients. When I made my anonymous inspection, after viewing the staff and decor, I made my excuses to leave. As I made for the exit door, I distinctly heard one of the ladies call out "Perv". Cheeky!!!

A sunbed and jacuzzi at Maxy's

Maxy's Sauna in Strood has superb decor and boasts a fine selection of young ladies now with the basic cost of massage at a reasonable £15.Before at £30 they were a bit pricey. Just along the A2, though now costing £20 is Platinum in Sittingbourne boasting yet more attractive young ladies.

CHATHAM - 01634

HEALTH & BODY WORLD ☆☆☆
2, Luton Rd. Ratings:A-6.B- .C-6.D-6.
Open: Mon-Sat 11-9.Sun 11-8. Tel. 405144. Basic Cost £15
Appearance: Staff friendly, young, versatile & racially varied.
Car Parking: Park further along Luton Rd.
Ladies: 2 from 6 different. Facilities: Sauna.

OASIS SAUNA & MASSAGE ☆☆☆
311A, High St. Ratings:A-6.B- .C-6.D-6.
Open: 11-9. Tel. 819173 Basic Cost £5
Appearance: Staff young, white, versatile & all shapes & sizes.
Car Parking: In a pedestrian area. Park at Brook St. end of High St.
Ladies: 2 from 6 different. Facilities: Sauna & Videos.

FOLKESTONE - 01303

DUO'S SPA & SAUNA ☆☆☆
27, Risborough Lane, Cheriton Ratings:A-5.B- .C-7.D-5.
Open 11-9. Tel.273730 Basic Cost £20
Appearance: Staff racially varied, versatile & all ages.
Car Parking: Park across the road in Taylor Rd.
Ladies: 2 from 10 different. Facilities: Sauna & Spa Bath.

SITTINGBOURNE - 01795

PLATINUM ☆☆☆☆
22, Church Rd., Central Park Stadium. Ratings:A-7.B- .C-9.D-8.
Open 24 hours a day, 7 days a week. Tel.426022. Basic Cost £20
Appearance: Staff racially varied, young & attractive, inc. Greek & Italian ladies.
Car Parking: On new industrial estate. Park outside.
Ladies: 3 from 5 different. Facilities: Sauna & Jacuzzi.

STROOD - 01634

MAXY'S SAUNA ☆☆☆☆☆
11A, Rochester Court, Anthony's Way. Ratings:A-8.B- .C-9.D-8.
Open 11-10. Tel. 722277 Basic Cost £15.
Appearance: Staff young, slim, racially varied & attractive, including ladies from Brazil and America.
Car Parking: On new industrial estate. Park outside.
Ladies: 3 to 6 from 10 different. Facilities: Sauna, Jacuzzi & Sunbed.

LANCASHIRE

Although Greater Manchester immediately to the south has a plethora of parlours, Lancashire is very poorly served. Indeed I could only find one in Blackpool & it simply had one lady working there. All in all a very disappointing county.

BLACKPOOL - 01253

PEACHES SAUNA ☆☆
52A, Cookson St Ratings:A-7.B- .C-5.D-5.
Open 10-8. Tel. 751520 Basic Cost: £20
Appearance: Staff young, white, versatile & larger than average.
Car Parking: Park around the corner in Milbourne St. or up the road.
Ladies: One lady Facilities: Sauna

LEICESTERSHIRE

In relation to its size, Leicestershire is probably better served with parlours than any other county in the land. Only the towns of Hinckley, Market Harborough & Melton Mowbray do not have one. And while a number are pretty ordinary, some are indeed first class establishments. Leicester as one might have expected has the most parlours, with fifteen in all. Most notable is Cleopatra's with a wealth of facilities and whilst the rooms are a little cluttered, the fifteen ladies working there are generally attractive , including in particular a very attractive tall blonde and include an international range with ladies from Greece, Italy, China, Puerto Rico & Malaysia. Across the road is Utopia with convenient access to its rear from the local N.C.P. car park and access to a licensed bar.

Heaven is to be found on the east side of the city in Green Lanes Rd..There one finds attractive staff, pleasant decor and unusually for the Midlands a totally mirrored room. Nearer the city centre is Flix in Humberstone Rd. with a pleasant selection of ladies in tasteful surroundings and a very charming receptionist.

Left
The King-sized jacuzzi at Utopia

Right
The waiting lounge at Flix

Also of note is Ladybirds in Narborough Rd.. The establishment boasts a choice of four ladies at any one time from a roster of 12 different. On entry one finds oneself in a pleasantly decorated open area off which are the massage rooms. The establishment also boasts a sauna and jacuzzi. Nearby in Braunstone Gate is Foxy's Sauna with attractive staff and soon to be refurbished, so do not be put off by the current state of the decor.

Out at Loughborough is to be found yet another of this country's many parlours called Oasis. The establishment could do with a bit better decoration but the staff more than make up for that small shortcoming.

The other town of particular note for parlours is the small town of Lutterworth. Amazingly, this town boasts two parlours, both of note. Peaches Studio which has been around longer is discreetly located on a top floor in Church St., near the town centre. Attractive staff also are to be found in the well appointed newer establishment Victoria House where one is made to feel welcome with Sky TV as one awaits ones massage.

In Coalville one should visit Silks where they offer a visiting massage service and the services of a male masseur if it is so required. Finally Shepshed boasts Edens a newly-opened establishment with attractive young staff & a fantasy room.

ASHBY-DE-LA-ZOUCH - 01530

TASHA'S ☆☆☆
60, Market St. Ratings:A-5.B- .C-8.D-5.
Open Mon-Fri 12-9.Sat 12-7. Tel. 412257 Basic Cost £10
Appearance: Staff young & versatile. One Chinese, one Asian.
Car Parking: Park outside in the street.
Ladies: 2 from 8 different Facilities: Sauna

COALVILLE - 01530

SILKS ☆☆☆☆
8, Hotel St. Ratings:A-7.B- .C-7.D-7.
Open 10-10 Tel. 817090 Basic Cost £10
Appearance: Staff racially varied, young & all shapes & sizes, including one lady from Sweden.
Car Parking: Park in free car park 100 yards down the road.
Ladies: 2 from 10 different. Facilities: Sauna, Jacuzzi, Videos, Sunbed & Steam Room

LEICESTER - 0116

ALANA'S ☆☆☆
28, Overton Rd. Ratings:A-6.B- .C-8.D-6.
Open Mon-Sat 12-10.Sun 12-9. Tel.246 0597 Basic Cost £5
Appearance: Staff young, versatile, white & presentable.
Car Parking: Park on pavement outside.
Ladies: 1 from 5 different Facilities:

CACHET HEALTH SALON ☆☆☆
633A, Saffron Lane Ratings:A-4.B- .C-7.D-5.
Open 11-9 Tel.283 7615 Basic Cost £5
Appearance: Staff white, cheerful & mature. One versatile. One Peruvian.
Car Parking: Park on pavement outside.
Ladies:1 from 7 different. Facilities: Sauna

CLEOPATRA'S ☆☆☆☆
18, Abbey St. Ratings:A-7.B-6.C-5.D-7.
Open 10.30-11.30 Tel.242 5885 Basic Cost £10
Appearance: Staff young, attractive & of many nationalities.
Car Parking: Park across road or across ring road in St. John St.
Ladies:3 from 15 different. Facilities: Sauna, Jacuzzi, Steam Room, Tanning Cab & Gym

DOLLYBIRDS ☆☆☆
55A, London Rd. Ratings:A-5.B- .C-7.D-6.
Open 11-10 Tel.255 6644 Basic Cost:£10
Appearance: Staff all shapes, sizes & ages, versatile & racially varied. One Chinese.
Car Parking: Park opposite or around the corner in Nelson St.
Ladies: 2 from 10 different. Facilities: Sauna & Videos.

EXECUTIVE SUITE ☆☆☆
69, Halford St. Ratings:A-5.B- .C-7.D-5.
Open Mon-Sat 10.30-10.Sun 12-10. Tel.251 2254. Basic Cost £10
Appearance: Staff young, white, versatile & shapely
Car Parking: Park opposite at the top of the street.
Ladies:2 or 3 from 12 different. Facilities: Sauna & Videos

FLIX ☆☆☆☆
8A, Humberstone Rd. Ratings:A-7.B- .C-6.D-5.
Open Mon-Fri 10.30-10.Sat 10.30-8.Sun 12-8. Tel.251 8039. Basic Cost £10
Appearance: Staff young, white, versatile & attractive. One half-Egyptian.
Car Parking: Park around the corner in Wimbledon St.
Ladies: 2 from 7 different. Facilities: Sauna, Jacuzzi & Spa Bath.

FOXY'S SAUNA ☆☆☆☆
77A,Braunstone Gate Ratings:A-7.B- .C-7.D-5.
Open Mon-Fri 10.30-10.Sat-Sun 10.30-8. Tel.255 8266 Basic Cost £10.
Appearance: Staff young, racially varied, versatile & shapely.
Car Parking: Park on opposite side of road 50 yards on.
Ladies:3 from 11 different Facilities: Sauna

HEAVEN ☆☆☆☆
189, Green Lane Rd. Ratings:A-7.B- .C-7.D-6.
Open 10-10 Tel. 246 4824 Basic Cost £10
Appearance: Staff white, young, versatile & all shapes & sizes.
Car Parking: Park outside or opposite in Spalding St.
Ladies: 2 from 8 different. Facilities: Sauna, Videos & Mirrored Room.

KESTRELS ☆☆
144, Checketts Rd. Ratings:A-4.B- .C-7.D-4.
Open Mon-Fri 12-6.30 Sat-Sun 12-6. Tel. 268 0266 Basic Cost £10.
Appearance: Staff white, cheerful, presentable & versatile. Mainly mature.
Car Parking: Park around the corner in Payne St.
Ladies: 2 from 5 different. Facilities: Sauna.

LACE ☆☆☆
204, Evington Rd. Ratings:A-7.B- .C-7.D-5.
Open 11-10.30 Tel. 273 0731 Basic Cost £10
Appearance: Staff young & all shapes & sizes. One half-Asian, one Italian.
Car Parking: Park across the road in Conway Rd.
Ladies: 2 from 6 different. Facilities: Videos.

LADYBIRDS ☆☆☆☆

196, Narborough Rd. Ratings:A-5.B- .C-8.D-6.

Open 10.30-10. Tel.254 4295 Basic Cost £10

Appearance: Staff youngish, white, versatile & all shapes & sizes.

Car Parking: Park across the road in Westleigh Rd.

Ladies: 4 from 12 different. Facilities: Sauna & Jacuzzi

PEACHES HEALTH STUDIO ☆☆☆

212, Melton Rd. Ratings:A-6.B- .C-8.D-5.

Open Mon-Sat 11-10. Tel. 268 0517 Basic Cost £10

Appearance: Staff youngish, white & mainly slim.

Car Parking: Park outside in road or across the road in St. Michael's Ave.

Ladies: 2 from 5 different. Facilities: Sauna & Sunbed.

PHOENIX ☆☆☆

101A, Kirby Rd. Ratings:A-6.B- .C-8.D-6.

Open Mon-Sat 11-8.30 Tel. 253 7888 Basic Cost £10

Appearance: Staff young, shapely, versatile & racially varied.

Car Parking: Park outside

Ladies: 1 or 2 from 6 different. Facilities: Videos.

RELAX ☆☆☆

60, Hinckley Rd. Ratings:A-7.B- .C-8.D-6 .

Open 12-12. Tel. 255 7531 Basic Cost £10

Appearance: Staff young, white & slim.

Car Parking: Park around the corner in Tyndale St.

Ladies: 1 lady Facilities:

UTOPIA ☆☆☆☆

15, Abbey St. Ratings:A-7.B- .C-5.D-6.

Open Mon-Sat 10-10.Sun 12-10 Tel. 262 1021 Basic Cost £10 DC.

Appearance: Staff mainly young, versatile & racially varied. One half-Spanish.

Car Parking: Use NCP car park off Belgrave Gate.

Ladies: 3 from 14 different. Facilities: Sauna, Jacuzzi, Sunbeds, Steam Room & Fantasy Room.

LOUGHBOROUGH - 01509

CLUB CLASSIQUE ☆☆☆
49A, Nottingham Rd. Ratings:A-6.B- .C-7.D-6.
Open 11-10. Tel. 610840 Basic Cost £10
Appearance: Staff white, young, versatile & shapely. One half-Italian.
Car Parking: Park around the corner in Bromhead St. where entrance is.
Ladies: 1 or 2 girls from 5 different. Facilities: Videos & Fantasy Room.

OASIS ☆☆☆☆
8, Leicester Rd. Ratings:A-7.B- .C-7.D-5.
Open 11-10 Tel. 212199 Basic Cost £10
Appearance: Staff racially varied, young, slim, presentable & versatile.
Car Parking: Park opposite down the road beyond the traffic lights.
Ladies: 3 from 7 different. Facilities: Sauna, Jacuzzi, Waterbed & Fantasy Room

LUTTERWORTH - 01455

PEACHES STUDIO ☆☆☆☆
31, Church St. Ratings:A-7.B-8.C-8.D-6.
Open Mon-Sat 12-8. Tel.550380 Basic Cost £12
Appearance: Staff white, youngish & versatile. One half-Malaysian.
Car Parking: Park outside in the road or around the corner in free car park.
Ladies: 2 from 5 different. Facilities: Sauna

VICTORIA HOUSE ☆☆☆☆
35, High St. Ratings:A-8.B-8.C-10.D-8.
Open 11-8. Tel. 559530 Basic Cost £12
Appearance: Staff cheerful, white, presentable & versatile. One half-Spanish.
Car Parking: Drive through archway & park at rear of premises.
Ladies: 2 from 7 different. Facilities: Sauna, Jacuzzi, Videos & Sky TV.

OAKHAM - 01572

SIMPLY THE BEST ☆☆☆
52, Dean St. Ratings:A-6.B- .C-7.D-5.
Open Mon-Fri 11-7.30.Sat-Sun 11-6.30 Tel.755119 Basic Cost £15.
Appearance: Staff white, versatile & all ages, shapes & sizes.
Car Parking: Park in road further down the street.
Ladies: 1 or 2 from 4 different. Facilities: Sauna & Videos.

SHEPSHED - 01509

EDENS ☆☆☆☆
61/63, Charnwood Rd. Ratings:A-7.B- .C-7.D-7.
Open Mon-Sat 12-9. Tel.508908 Basic Cost £10
Appearance: Staff young, shapely & versatile. One Asian.
Car Parking: Park opposite in Garendon Rd. Entrance at side.
Ladies: 2 from 6 different. Facilities: Sauna, Jacuzzi, Videos & Fantasy Room

WIGSTON - 0116

WIGSTON SAUNA & SOLARIUM ☆☆☆
89, Blaby Rd. Ratings:A-7.B- .C-6.D-7.
Open 12-10. Tel.277 0266 Basic Cost £10
Appearance: Staff young, racially varied, versatile & all shapes & sizes.
Car Parking: Park around the corner in Glengate or Albion St.
Ladies:1 from 7 different. Facilities: Sauna, Videos, Sunbed & Fantasy Room.

MERSEYSIDE

Again a disappointing county, particularly when compared to its neighbour Greater Manchester. There are three studios on either side of the Mersey, but none stand out. Perhaps the best is The Studio in Prescot Rd., Liverpool, which has attractive staff & is tastefully decorated. The entrance, however, leaves a lot to be desired and would put most visitors off before they ventured further into the establishment.

Probably the most notable parlour is the unusually located Surfers in Haydock situated in a commercial premises behind a garage. It is so named because it boasts a waterbed, supposedly giving one something other than the ubiquitous Internet on which to surf.

BOOTLE - 0151

FIRST CHOICE ☆☆☆
First Floor, 1, Canal St. Ratings:A-6.B- .C-8.D-6.
Open Mon-Sat 11-9.Sun 11-7. Tel. 933 9248. Basic Cost £10
Appearance: Staff youngish, white, versatile & all shapes & sizes. One half-Brazilian.
Car Parking: Park outside.
Ladies: 2 from 10 different. Facilities: Jacuzzi

HAYDOCK - 01925

SURFERS ☆☆☆☆

Rear of Haydock Island Motors, Ashton Rd. Ratings:A-7.B- .C-8.D-7.

Open Mon-Sat 11-9.Sun 11-8. Tel. 220070 Basic Cost £10

Appearance: Staff white, youngish, versatile & all shapes & sizes.

Car Parking: Located in building labelled P.S.M. Park on premises.

Ladies: 2 from 12 different. Facilities: Sauna, Jacuzzi & Waterbed.

LIVERPOOL - 0151

The STUDIO ☆☆☆☆

396, Prescot Rd. Ratings:A-7.B- .C-7.D-5.

Open 10-10 Tel. 220 2023 Basic Cost £10

Appearance: Staff white, youngish, cheerful & versatile.

Car Parking: Park around the corner in Ennismore Rd.

Ladies: 3 from 11 different. Facilities: Sauna & Videos.

TWILIGHT ZONE ☆☆☆

2A, Parton St. Ratings:A-6.B- .C-7.D-7.

Open 12-10. Tel. 261 0570 Basic Cost £5 A/V

Appearance: Staff racially varied, youngish & versatile.

Car Parking: Park outside. Vehicular access to street is from Ottley St.

Ladies: 2 from 8 different. Facilities: Videos & Steam Box.

SOUTH WIRRAL - 0151

PARADISE ☆☆☆

Flat over Fantasia,365,Chester Rd., Little Sutton. Ratings:A-6.B- .C-8.D-5.

Open 11-9. Tel 339 1977 Basic Cost £10

Appearance: Staff young, white, versatile & mainly shapely.

Car Parking: Use free car park behind building in Smithy Court.

Ladies: 2 from 10 different. Facilities: Fantasy Room.

RASCALS ☆☆☆

1, Lower Mersey St., Ellesmere Port. Ratings:A-6.B- .C-8.D-5.

Open 11-9 Tel. 355 2749 Basic Cost £10

Appearance: Staff young, versatile & racially varied.

Car parking: Park opposite.

Ladies: 1 from 6 different. Facilities: Videos, Herbal Bath & Fantasy Room

WIRRAL - 0151

The CABIN ☆☆

122, New Chester Rd., New Ferry. Ratings:A-4.B- .C-7.D-5.

Open 12-9. Tel. 645 5754 Basic Cost £10

Appearance: Staff mature, white, friendly & versatile.

Car Parking: Park opposite in Mayfields North.

Ladies: 1 or 2 from 3 different. Facilities:

NORTH YORKSHIRE

Curiously, once one moves north of this county one begins to enter the no man's land of massage. I could find no parlours in Cleveland, Cumbria, Co. Durham, Northumberland or even the metropolitan county of Tyne & Wear. On the massage front Manchester United beats Newcastle United by 50 odd - Nil. So on a trip north after you leave this county you find nothing until you reach Edinburgh & Glasgow.

Not that North Yorks has an inordinate number of parlours of which to boast. But there are three - two in York, the Sun Sauna Centre boasts an attractive selection of young ladies in a clean tidy establishment. Further there is one in Yorkshire's answer to Tunbridge Wells - Harrogate. Cold Bath Rd. is a pleasant, certainly respectable area of town, and La Rochelle, under the same management as Chantilly in Bradford and Ladybirds in Leeds, while providing fairly basic rooms, has a fine selection of staff. Now that our ex-chancellor looks like becoming the local M.P. at the next election he could do worse than give a little bit of business to a local small business in his constituency by indulging in a massage.

HARROGATE - 01423

LA ROCHELLE ☆☆☆☆

129, Cold Bath Rd. Ratings:A-7.B-6.C-7.D-6.

Open: Mon-Sat 10-9.30.Sun 10-8.30. Tel.507761 Basic Cost £10

Appearance: Staff all ages, racially varied & attractive, inc. ladies from Germany & Australia.

Car Parking: Park around the corner in Queen's Rd.

Ladies: 3 from 6 different Facilities: Sauna

YORK - 01904

KWIKTAN SAUNA ☆☆

26, Market St. Ratings:A-5.B- .C-3.D-6.

Open: Mon-Fri 11-8.30.Sat 11-6. Tel. 621847. Basic Cost £10

Appearance: Staff mature, white & cheerful.

Car Parking: Difficult in the city. Use pay & display in Piccadilly.

Ladies: 2 from 7 different. Facilities: Sauna & Sunbeds.

SUN SAUNA CENTRE ☆☆☆☆
1, Little Stonegate Ratings:A-6.B- .C-3.D-7.
Open:11-6.30 Tel.613116. Basic Cost £15
Appearance: Staff young, slim, racially varied & versatile.
Car Parking: Difficult in the city. Use pay & display in Bootham Row.
Ladies: 1 from 5 different. Facilities: Sauna

NORTHAMPTONSHIRE

As one moves south one finds the price of a massage rises & curiously it is here in the southernmost Midland county that prices reach their peak. At no parlour does the price of a basic body massage drop below £15. Indeed at one establishment - the estimable Thai House in Kettering Rd. the price for a basic massage rises to £30, though one can use Access or Visa. They also have very pleasant hydrobaths and as the name of the parlour indicates a fair number of ladies working there that hail from Thailand.

Also of note in the county town are two other parlours. The best run parlour in Northampton is probably St. James Health Spa. The facilities are excellent and the staff generally attractive, their photos adorn the wall by the sauna. But one should not forget Studio 171 at 171, Kettering Rd. The staff here are perhaps even more attractive than at St. James and the establishment is very tastefully decorated.

Left
The jacuzzi at St. James Health Spa

Right
A massage room at Studio 171

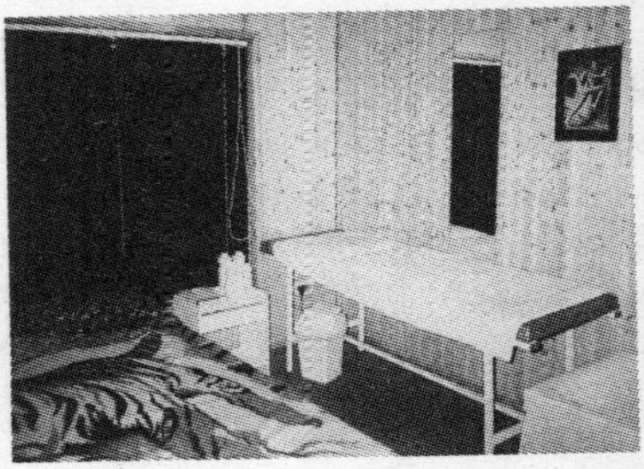

In the small town of Rushden there are two parlours practically next door to one another, both with unusual costs - £17.50 & £18.50, maybe they include an element of V.A.T.

Finally, unusually the A14 Studio in Burton Latimer has a Swedish lady working there who looks very Mediterranean - almost a contradiction in terms!!

BURTON LATIMER - 01536

A14 STUDIO ☆☆☆☆
160B, High St. Ratings:A-5.B-8.C-9.D-6.
Open: Mon-Fri 10-10.Sat 11-7. Tel. 420219 Basic Cost £16
Appearance: Staff mature, cheerful, white & versatile. One Swedish.
Car Parking: Park outside in the street.
Ladies: 3 from 10 different. Facilities: Sauna, Jacuzzi, Videos & Steam Room.

NORTHAMPTON - 01604

ALTERNATIVE HEALTH CENTRE ☆☆
88A, Wellingborough Rd. Ratings:A-5.B- .C-5.D-5.
Open: Mon, Tues, Fri & Sat 10.30-6.Wed-Thu 10.30-9. Tel.29248. Basic Cost £25
Appearance: Staff white, youngish & presentable
Car Parking: Park opposite in Portland Place
Ladies: 2 from 6 different. Facilities:

ST. JAMES HEALTH SPA ☆☆☆☆
38, Ambush St. Ratings:A-7.B- .C-9.D-7.
Open Mon-Fri 10-10.Sat 10-7. Tel.585452 Basic Cost £25
Appearance: Staff white, versatile, attractive and all shapes, sizes & ages.
Car Parking: Park outside.
Ladies: 2 from 6 different. Facilities: Jacuzzi, Sunbed, Sauna & Fantasy Room.

SOFT TOUCH BODY WORKS ☆☆☆
Media House, St. James Mill Rd. Ratings:A-6.B- .C-9.D-6.
Open Mon-Fri 10.30-8.Sat 12-6. Tel.752390. Basic Cost £25
Appearance: Staff white, all ages, personable & generally slim.
Car Parking: An Industrial Unit. Park outside.
Ladies: 5 from 6 different. Facilities: Hydrobath & Sunbed.

STUDIO 171 ☆☆☆☆
171, Kettering Rd. Ratings:A-7.B- .C-6.D-7.
Open Mon-Fri 10-10. Sat 11-6. Tel 604627. Basic Cost £20
Appearance: Staff young, white, versatile & generally slimmish.
Car Parking: Park outside or in one of the roads opposite.
Ladies: 2 from 4 different. Facilities: Sauna, Whirlpool, Videos & Sunbed.

THAI HOUSE ☆☆☆☆
104, Kingsley Park Terrace, Kettering Rd. Ratings:A-7.B-7.C-6.D-7.
Open Mon-Fri 10.30-10.Sat-Sun 10.30-6. Tel.720066. Basic Cost £30
Appearance: Staff young, all shapes & sizes - half Thai, half white.
Car Parking: Park in front or around the corner in Moore St.
Ladies: 7 from 12 different. Facilities: Hydrobaths

RUSHDEN - 01933

MASAHA
122A, High St. Ratings:A- .B- .C- 7.D-6.
Open Mon-Fri 10-9.Sat 10-5.Tel. 317239 Basic Cost £17.50.
Appearance: Money required up front. Staff apparently young, white & versatile.
Car Parking: Park outside or around the corner in Victoria Rd.
Ladies: 1 from 4 different. Facilities: Sauna & Solarium

STUDIO K ☆☆☆
126A, High St. Ratings:A-5.B- .C-7.D-5.
Open Mon-Fri 10-7.Sat 10-5. Tel. 315798 Basic Cost £18.50
Appearance: Staff mature, white & slimmish.
Car Parking: Park outside or around the corner in Victoria Rd.
Ladies: 1 from 3 different. Facilities: Sauna & Sunbed

NOTTINGHAMSHIRE

The County of Robin Hood might seem an appropriate place for an occupation of a somewhat unconventional kind, but you would be mistaken, for like Merseyside this county with a not inconsiderable urban population disappoints.

In all I could only find 5 parlours. Indeed in neighbouring Ilkeston, Sandiacre & Long Eaton I could find more, perhaps the authorities in neighbouring Derbyshire are more generous in their view of such establishments.

The only notable parlour in Nottingham is Palm Beach, where the premises are clean, the ladies attractive and generally amenable to requests for more unusual kinds of massage.

What is more of the five parlours the one of most note was curiously not located in Nottingham where the other four were but in the quiet village of Huthwaite, near Sutton-in-Ashfield.

Nero's Health Centre used to boast a regrettably slightly tatty exterior though it always more than made up for it inside. Its extensive facilities include, in addition to the standard sauna & jacuzzi, a steam bath, sunbeds, a needle shower, free refreshments & papers while you await, as well as every 10th massage free, and a choice of three lovely ladies. The exterior is now much improved - an all around success story.

Nero's

Left
The exterior

Right
The King-sized jacuzzi

NOTTINGHAM - 0115

GENESIS II ☆☆☆
28, Park Rd. Ratings:A-5.B- .C-7.D-6.
Open Mon-Fri 11-9.Sat 11-7.Sun 12-9. Tel. 950 9185 Basic Cost £15
Appearance: Staff white and all ages, shapes & sizes.
Car Parking: Park outside or opposite.
Ladies: 3 from 6 different. Facilities: Sauna

PALM BEACH ☆☆☆☆
Excise Chambers, 31, Pelham St. Ratings:A-6.B- .C-3.D-6.
Open 11-8. Tel. 952 7757 Basic Cost £10
Appearance: Staff young, racially varied, versatile, slim & presentable, including one lady from Italy.
Car Parking: Difficult in city centre. Find a free spot anywhere near.
Ladies: 2 from 5 different. Facilities: Sauna & Sunbed

SPANGLES ☆☆☆
Rear of 351,Derby Rd. Ratings:A-7.B- .C-9.D-6.
Open Mon-Fri 12-8. Sat 12-6. Tel. 979 1901. Basic Cost £12.50
Appearance: Staff young, white & all shapes and sizes. One Portuguese.
Car Parking: Above block of shops. Park at rear.
Ladies: 2 from 4 different. Facilities: Sauna

SUTTON-IN-ASHFIELD - 01623

NERO'S HEALTH CENTRE ☆☆☆☆☆
27, Main St., Huthwaite. Ratings:A-7.B- .C-8.D-7.
Open 11-9 Tel. 550383 Basic Cost £20
Appearance: Staff youngish, racially varied & attractive.
Car Parking: Park outside in the street.
Ladies: 3 from 10 different. Facilities: Sauna, Jacuzzi, Sunbed & Needle Shower

SHROPSHIRE

Although a basically rural county Shropshire's four parlours do the county proud. Three are located in Shrewsbury, and one has now reopened in Telford. It is not particularly notable.

Shrewsbury's three are pretty basic without even a sauna or a jacuzzi, but the lasses working there will take good care of you. In particular the best of the three is probably Rachel's Health Studio in Frankwell. The staff there are particularly effervescent. You have been warned!!!

SHREWSBURY - 01743

RACHEL'S HEALTH STUDIO ☆☆☆☆
13, Frankwell Ratings:A-8.B- .C-6.D-6.
Open Mon-Sat 12-8. Tel.359995 Basic Cost £10
Appearance: Staff youngish, white, attractive, versatile and all shapes & sizes.
Car Parking: Park by the roundabout at the end of Frankwell.
Ladies: 1 from 4 different. Facilities:

SUPREME MASSAGE ☆☆☆
57, Coton Hill Ratings:A-7.B- .C-7.D-6.
Open 11-9. Tel.236553 Basic Cost £10
Appearance: Staff young, racially varied & versatile. One Malaysian.
Car Parking: Park on opposite side of road by river.
Ladies: 1 from 6 different. Facilities:

A TOUCH OF CLASS ☆☆☆
3/5, Coffee House Passage Ratings:A-6.B-6.C-2.D-5.
Open Mon-Sat 10.30-7.30 Tel. 241499 Basic Cost £15
Appearance: Staff youngish, slim, racially varied & versatile.
Car Parking: Before 6 you must use a voucher from a local newsagent to park.
Ladies: 1 from 5 different. Facilities:

TELFORD - 01952

PENTHOUSE ☆☆
21, Tan Bank, Wellington Ratings:A-5.B- .C-5.D-5.
Open 11-8. Tel. 223834 Basic Cost:
Appearance: Staff white, all ages, shapes & sizes
Car Parking: Two pay & display car parks nearby.
Ladies: 1or 2 from 6 different. Facilities:

SOMERSET

Another rural county and again an interesting selection of parlours. Apparently both Taunton & Yeovil have boasted parlours in the past but now the county's choice is restricted to two in Bridgwater and one in Wellington.

The most notable is Dawn's in Bridgwater. On my first visit to the establishment I was not able to come to a considered view of it, but the ladies working there basically struck me as friendly and unusually they offer all potential clients free drinks of an alcoholic nature while you are waiting to make your choice of masseuse. One has a first-class choice.

Also notable is Cleo's in Wellington. Like their sister establishment - Park House in Bristol - they operate a curious closed on Wednesday policy. However the staff are presentable and all ages.

Finally Eve's, also in Bridgwater not only has versatile staff, but a fantasy room in which to demonstrate their versatility. For a small predominantly rural county - not a bad selection.

BRIDGWATER - 01278

DAWNS ☆☆☆☆
2, Silver St. Ratings:A-7.B- .C-7.D-6.
Open 10.30-10.30 Tel. 450588 Basic Cost £8
Appearance: Staff all shapes and sizes, racially varied & versatile.
Car Parking: Park around the corner by the church in St. Mary St.
Ladies: 3 from 10 different. Facilities: Corner Bath & Complimentary Bar.

EVE'S ☆☆☆
3, New Rd. Ratings:A-6.B- .C-6.D-5.
Open 10.30-10 Tel. 446474 Basic Cost:
Appearance: Staff white, cheerful, friendly, versatile & all ages.
Car Parking: Park opposite or around the corner at the top of the road.
Ladies: 2 from 5 different. Facilities: Videos & Fantasy Room.

WELLINGTON - 01823

CLEO'S ☆☆☆☆
37, Fore St. Ratings:A-7.B- .C-6.D-6.
Open: Mon, Tues, Thurs & Fri 10.30-7 . Tel.660515. Basic Cost:
Appearance: Staff all ages, racially varied & versatile. One Russian.
Car Parking: Park outside or opposite.
Ladies: 2 or 3 from 6 different. Facilities: Jacuzzi & Videos.

SOUTH YORKSHIRE

South Yorkshire, or more to the point Sheffield where most of the parlours are, besides being host to the World Snooker Championship, is also host to an almost unmatchable array of massage parlours. Indeed in the Attercliffe Rd., there are more parlours than in any other road in the entire country. Although only one of the five is outstanding and there an unfortunately large number of establishments keener on taking your money than letting you have some idea of what you are paying for, Sheffield probably boasts the best value in massage parlours in Britain. Prices are generally lower, but that does not mean all the parlours are flea pits.

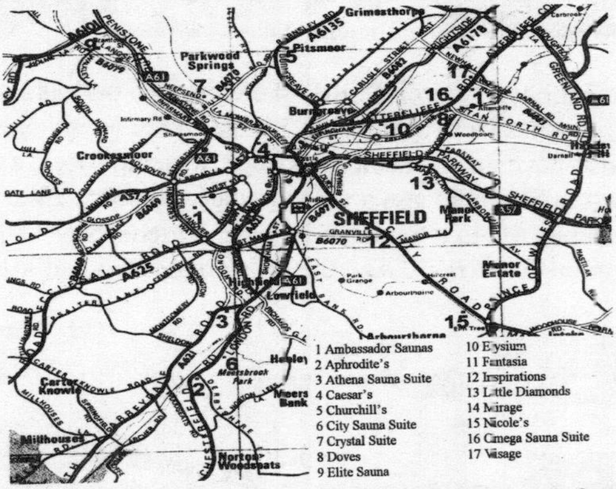

Indeed at Caesars, for example, entry only costs £4, yet for that small sum, one has access to a sauna, an adult video lounge and a large scale jacuzzi as well the delights of a full body massage. Furthermore, particularly after 11p.m. they have as many as 8 lovely ladies and I do mean lovely.

Caesar's

Left
The exterior

Right
The V.I.P.
room

And Caesars is not alone. At Ambassadors Sauna there are a lovely selection of ladies, a pool room, a fully equipped fantasy room & unusually a decent-sized swimming pool. The Crystal Suite in Neepsend Lane, long established, has secure parking, as well as a bar, sauna, steam room & jacuzzi. Entrance there is only £6.

Crystal Suite

Left
The exterior

Right
The waiting lounge

In the above-mentioned Attercliffe Rd., there are two parlours of note - Omega Sauna Suite, which with between 3 & 7 ladies there at any one time must be worth a visit. They also have an amusements lounge, a steam room, a jacuzzi they claim to be the biggest in Sheffield and a video lounge with Sky TV. Also the Elysium, here the facilities run to a Sauna, a Jacuzzi, Videos, Sky TV, A Pool Table, Sunbeds and a Fantasy Room. And the girls are not too bad looking either.

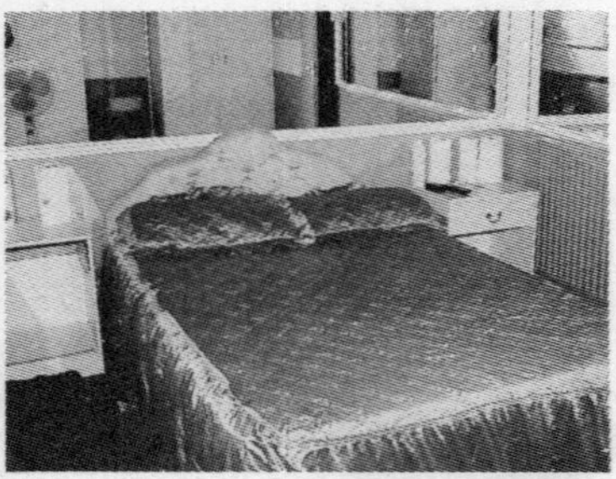

Omega Sauna Suite

Left
The V.I.P. room

Right
The biggest jacuzzi in Sheffield??

Finally, outside Sheffield, there several parlours worth visiting. Doncaster boasts the 155 Sauna Suite at 155, Balby Rd. Here there are an attractive range of staff including one lady from Singapore, plus Sauna & Videos.

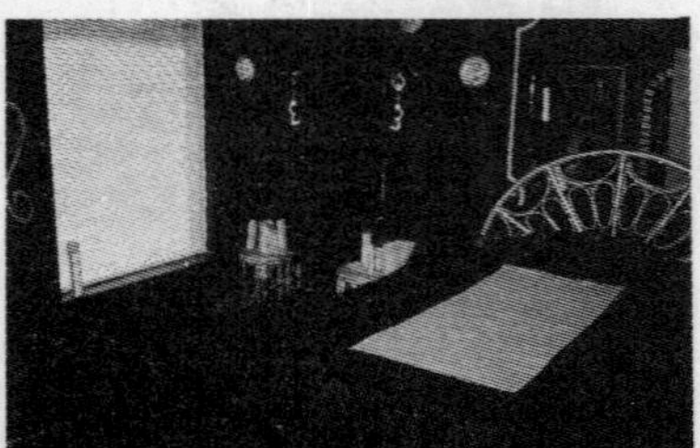

The principle massage room at Mons Venus

At 55a, Copley Rd., Mons Venus has an attractive selection of ladies in tastefully newly decorated surroundings. The staff are young, attractive and white and the establishment boasts a four poster bed as well as full fantasy facilities, soon to be connected to the entrance lobby by a spiral staircase.

Last but not least, Rotherham, or to be more precise, Maltby boasts, discreetly tucked away above a furniture shop, Chequers. Here besides the existence of the only instance of one being able to win a massage as a prize on a fruit machine, this establishment boasts Sauna, Jacuzzi, Videos, Sunbed, Four Poster Bed, Fantasy Room & a Stoneroom in the basement. It is amazing how they have managed to fit it all in.

Chequers

Left
The fruit machine

Right
The Stoneroom

DONCASTER - 01302

MONS VENUS ☆☆☆☆
55A, Copley Rd. Ratings:A-7.B- .C-6.D-7 .
Open 10-9. Tel. 340902. Basic Cost £5.
Appearance: Staff young, racially varied, versatile & generally attractive.
Car Parking: Entrance is in Montague St. Park there.
Ladies: 2 from 6 different. Facilities: Stoneroom, Fantasy Room, Videos & Four Poster Bed.

155 SAUNA SUITE ☆☆☆☆
155, Balby Rd. Ratings:A-7.B- .C-10.D-7.
Open Mon-Fri 10-4.Sat-Sun 12-4. Tel. 858155 Basic Cost £10.
Appearance: Staff young, racially varied, versatile & all shapes & sizes. One lady is from Singapore.
Car Parking: Park on premises.
Ladies: 2 from 11 different. Facilities: Sauna, Videos & Steam Room.

<u>ROTHERHAM - 01709</u>

CHEQUERS ☆☆☆☆☆
232, Rotherham Rd., Maltby Ratings:A-8.B- .C-9.D-7.
Open Mon-Fri 12-8.Sat 12-6 Tel. 817270 Basic Cost £5
Appearance: Staff young, slim, attractive & very versatile
Car Parking: Park at rear of premises where entrance is.
Ladies:2 from 8 different. Facilities: Sauna, Jacuzzi, Videos, Four poster bed, Sunbed, Fantasy Room & Stoneroom.

<u>SHEFFIELD - 0114</u>

AMBASSADOR SAUNAS ☆☆☆☆
37, Cavendish St. Ratings:A-7.B- .C-7.D-8.
Open 10-12 Tel 272 4461 Basic Cost £8
Appearance: Staff versatile and all ages, races, shapes & sizes.
Car Parking: Park outside or down the road
Ladies: 4 from 12 different. Facilities: Sauna, Fantasy Room, Videos, Pool Room & Swimming Pool

APHRODITE'S ☆☆☆
271,Chesterfield Rd. Ratings:A-5.B- .C-6.D-4.
Open 10-8. Tel. 281 2829 Basic Cost £5
Appearance: Staff all ages, shapes & sizes, racially varied & versatile.
Car Parking: Park around the corner in Millmount Rd.
Ladies: 3 from 12 different. Facilities: Videos & Fantasy Room

ATHENA SAUNA SUITE
117, Wolseley Rd. Ratings:A- .B- .C-7.D- .
Open 24 hours a day Tel. 258 9814 Basic Cost £6
Appearance: Money required up front. Staff apparently versatile & racially varied.
Car Parking: Park outside or around the corner in Abbeydale Rd.
Ladies: 2 or 3 from 12 different Facilities: Sauna & Videos.

CAESARS ☆☆☆☆☆
32, Corporation St. Ratings:A-8.B-7.C-7.D-8.
Open 24 hours a day Tel. 275 5219 Basic Cost £4
Appearance: Staff youngish, generally attractive & racially varied.
Car Parking: Park in private car park at corner of Spring St. & Workhouse Lane.
Ladies: 2 to 8 from 30 different. Facilities: Sauna, Jacuzzi, Videos, Pool Room & Steam Room

CHURCHILLS ☆☆☆
184, Barnsley Rd. Ratings:A-6.B- .C-7.D-5.
Open 10-12. Tel. 256 1032 Basic Cost £5 A/V
Appearance: Staff mature, very versatile & racially varied.
Car Parking: Park around the corner in Firshill Close
Ladies: 3 from 12 different. Facilities: Sauna, Videos & Fantasy Room

CITY SAUNA SUITE ☆☆☆
97, Chesterfield Rd. Ratings:A-5.B- .C-7.D-8.
Open 10-10.30 Tel. 258 1103 Basic Cost £8
Appearance: Staff youngish, racially varied & versatile. One half-African, half-Italian.
Car Parking: Park around the corner in Meersbrook Park Rd.
Ladies: 3 from 15 different. Facilities: Sauna, Videos, Sunbeds, Steam Room & Pool Table

CRYSTAL SUITE ☆☆☆☆☆
144, Neepsend Lane Ratings:A-7.B- .C-10.D-7.
Open 10-2 Tel. 275 2977 Basic Cost £6
Appearance: Staff young, attractive, racially varied & versatile. One is Filipino.
Car Parking: Park on premises.
Ladies: 3 to 5 from 15 different. Facilities: Sauna, Jacuzzi, Videos, Bar & Steam Room

DOVES ☆☆
548, Attercliffe Rd. Ratings:A-4.B- .C-7.D-4.
Open 10-12 Tel. 261 1234 Basic Cost
Appearance: Staff young, slimmish, racially varied & versatile.
Car Parking: Park across the road in Heppenstall Lane.
Ladies: 2 from 12 different. Facilities: Sauna & Videos.

ELITE SAUNA ☆☆☆
398, Langsett Rd. Ratings:A-7.B- .C-9.D-6.
Open Mon-Fri 10-10.Sat 10-8.Sun 12-8. Tel. 285 4004 Basic Cost
Appearance: Staff mature, racially varied & versatile.
Car Parking: Park at rear of premises by entrance.
Ladies: 3 or 4 from 6 different. Facilities: Sauna, Videos, Sunbed & Sky TV.

ELYSIUM ☆☆☆☆
160, Attercliffe Rd. Ratings:A-6.B-6.C-9.D-5.
Open Sun-Wed 10-4.Thu-Sat 10-6. Tel. 275 4472 Basic Cost £5
Appearance: Staff very versatile & all ages, shapes, races & sizes, including one lady from Egypt.
Car Parking: Turn into Warren St. & park at rear by entrance.
Ladies: 3 to 5 from 12 different. Facilities: Sauna, Jacuzzi, Videos, Sunbed, Pool Table, Fantasy Room & Sky TV.

FANTASIA ☆☆☆
728, Attercliffe Rd. Ratings:A-6.B- .C-7.D-5.
Open Mon-Sat 10-8.30.Sun 12-8.Tel. 244 3853 Basic Cost
Appearance: Staff youngish, white & versatile.
Car Parking: Free car park around the corner in Bodmin St.
Ladies: 2 from 5 different. Facilities: Videos

INSPIRATIONS ☆☆☆
202, City Rd. Ratings:A-6.B- .C-8.D-5.
Open Mon-Sat 12-8. Tel. 270 0794 Basic Cost £10
Appearance: Staff friendly, slim, versatile, one young, one mature.
Car Parking: Park outside or opposite.
Ladies: 2 different. Facilities: Videos & Fantasy Room

LITTLE DIAMONDS ☆☆
Manor Lane, Nunnery Drive Ind. Est. Ratings:A-5.B- .C-8.D-5.
Open 10-8 Tel. 275 3157 Basic Cost
Appearance: Staff racially varied, youngish & very versatile.
Car Parking: On Industrial Estate. Park opposite.
Ladies: 2 or 3 from 10 different. Facilities: Sauna, Videos & Fantasy Room.

MIRAGE ☆☆☆
291, Sheffield Rd., Tinsley Ratings:A-6.B- .C-8.D-5.
Open Mon-Sat 10-11.30.Sun 12-9. Tel.244 3432 Basic Cost £5
Appearance: Staff youngish, racially varied & versatile.
Car Parking: Park at rear of shops between parlour & motorway.
Ladies: 3 from 12 different. Facilities: Sauna & Videos.

NICOLE'S ☆☆☆
714, City Rd. Ratings:A-5.B- .C-6.D-5.
Open Mon-Sat 10-8.Sun 11-7. Tel. 253 0340 Basic Cost
Appearance: Staff youngish, white & versatile.
Car Parking: Park across the road in Wulfric Rd.
Ladies: 2 from 9 different. Facilities: Videos.

OMEGA SAUNA SUITE ☆☆☆☆☆
653, Attercliffe Rd. Ratings:A-7.B- .C-7.D-5.
Open 24 hours a day Tel. 244 7196 Basic Cost £8
Appearance: Staff racially varied, youngish & versatile including Arab, Somali & White South African ladies.
Car Parking: Park around the corner in Baker St.
Ladies: 7 from 30 different. Facilities: Sauna, Jacuzzi & Videos.

VISAGE ☆☆☆
761, Attercliffe Rd. Ratings:A-6.B- .C-8.D-5.
Open 24 hours a day Tel. 261 7625 Basic Cost
Appearance: Staff mature, friendly & moderately attractive.
Car Parking: Park next door outside Barclay's Bank.
Ladies: 2 from 10 different. Facilities: Sauna & Videos.

STAFFORDSHIRE

In other words the Potteries or to be more precise Stoke-on-Trent is where all of Staffordshire's parlours are located. There are none I could find in Cannock, Burton, Tamworth or even next-door Newcastle.

And within the six towns, although all except Hanley are represented, of the city's fourteen parlours, five are in Stoke & three in Burslem, leaving only two apiece in Fenton, Longton & Tunstall.

The parlours of Stoke have improved over the past six months or so, since I first looked the area over. As earlier this year Memories is a tidy, clean establishment with attractive & friendly staff. Unfortunately Bel-Air also in Tunstall has deteriorated somewhat, not unexpectedly when one considers they have moved twice within their industrial estate.

The most notable improvement has been by Rachael's in Stoke. It has vacated its old premises in Hartshill Rd. and has moved into the old premises of Fingertips in Glebe St., also occupying the premises next door. Technically it occupies both 15 and 15A Glebe St. and the transformation since the days of Fingertips, possibly the most unattractive parlour in the country in its time, is remarkable. It now boasts first class facilities, attractive staff, friendly management and tasteful decor - almost worthy of 5-star status.

But I feel I was also a little unfair to several other parlours, and having revisited them lately I have come to the conclusion that three other parlours are also worthy of 4-star status - Adele's, C.J.'s and Stella's. Furthermore the newly opened Guys 'n' Dolls in Stoke is also worth so honouring.

Stella's has friendly management, very reasonable facilities, given the compact nature of the premises and attractive staff. Moreover the decor is extremely pleasant.

Adele's is run by a lady who used to run a fish 'n' chip shop, so she should know how to take care of her clientele. I was impressed by the way she takes care of her staff, who I am sure reciprocate by taking care of the customers. The facilities are limited but the place is clean, tidy and pleasantly decorated. The staff also include some beauties.

C.J.'s is run by the ladies who used to run Bel-Air when it was Xanadu and although they have only just arrived there, they promise to make the place as pleasant to visit as Xanadu was. To that aim, they will have made some additions to the old facilities at Cindy's - its previous name - and a four-star parlour will be the result.

Finally although Guys 'n' Dolls is pretty basic, with no notable extra facilities, the ladies are friendly and attractive. On entry one finds a pleasant waiting lounge. Upstairs the three massage rooms are clean and tidy.

STOKE-ON-TRENT - 01782

ADDICTION ☆
223, Newcastle St., Burslem Ratings:A-3.B- .C-8.D-4.
Open Mon-Fri 10-10. Sat 11-8.Sun 12-9. Tel. 832623 Basic Cost £8
Appearance: Staff versatile, racially varied, all ages, shapes & sizes. One is half-Italian.
Car Parking: Entry at rear near free Car Park in Reid St.
Ladies: 2 from 6 different. Facilities:

ADELE'S ☆☆☆☆
81, King St., Fenton Ratings:A-7.B- .C-6.D-6.
Open Mon-Sat 10-10.Sun 12-9. Tel. 744152 Basic Cost £8
Appearance: Staff racially varied, versatile, presentable & all ages, shapes & sizes. Again one is half-Italian
Car Parking: Park around the back of the premises in Fenpark Rd.
Ladies: 3 from 10 different Facilities:

BALMORAL ☆☆
60, Liverpool Rd., Stoke Ratings:A-4.B- .C-6.D-5.
Open 10-10 Tel. 844475 Basic Cost £5
Appearance: Staff white, versatile, all ages & generally shapely.
Car Parking: Park across the road in Bamber St.
Ladies: 2 from 7 different. Facilities:

BEL-AIR ☆☆☆
380, High St., Tunstall Ratings:A-5.B- .C-7.D-4.
Open Mon-Thu 11-11.Fri-Sun 11-7.30. Tel. 832638. Basic Cost £7
Appearance: Staff youngish, versatile & white.
Car Parking: Park within nearby Longus Industrial estate
Ladies: 2 from 9 different. Facilities: Sauna & Videos

C.J.'S ☆☆☆☆
Crown House, Old Mill St., Stoke. Ratings:A-7.B- .C-7.D-7.
Open Mon-Fri 11-11.Sat-Sun 11-8. Tel. 747955. Basic Cost £7
Appearance: Staff polite, versatile, racially varied & all ages, shapes & sizes.
Car Parking: Park in front just off City Rd.
Ladies: 2 or 3 from 10 different. Facilities: Sunbed, Jacuzzi & Videos.

GENEVIEVE'S ☆☆

12, Brickhouse St., Burslem Ratings:A-4.B-5.C-5.D-4.

Open 11-10.15 Tel. 837213 Basic Cost £7

Appearance: Staff young, busty, versatile & racially varied.

Car Parking: Park across the road in Market Place

Ladies: 2 from 8 different. Facilities: Sauna & Jacuzzi

GUYS 'N' DOLLS ☆☆☆☆

58, Epworth St., Stoke Ratings:A-7.B- .C-7.D-6.

Open Mon-Sat 11-8 Tel. 417003 Basic Cost £6

Appearance: Staff all ages, versatile & racially varied, including one lady from Mexico.

Car Parking: Park further along the street.

Ladies: 3 from 10 different. Facilities:

KELLY'S ☆☆

51, Newcastle St., Burslem Ratings:A-5.B- .C-6.D-4.

Open Mon-Fri 11-11. Sat-Sun 10.30-10.15 Tel. 837811 Basic Cost £6

Appearance: Staff racially varied, versatile & all ages. shapes & sizes. One Thai.

Car Parking: Entry at rear. Park across the road in Blake St.

Ladies: 2 from 10 different. Facilities: Jacuzzi & Videos.

MEMORIES ☆☆☆☆

14, High St., Tunstall Ratings:A-7.B- .C-7.D-6.

Open 10- 10.30 Tel. 811487 Basic Cost £5

Appearance: Staff presentable, racially varied & versatile.

Car Parking: Park around the back in Pinnox St.

Ladies: 2 from 10 different. Facilities:

RACHAEL'S ☆☆☆☆

15, Glebe St., Stoke Ratings:A-7.B- .C-7.D-7.

Open 10-10 Tel. 749237 Basic Cost £8

Appearance: Staff all ages, shapes and sizes, racially varied & versatile.

Car Parking: Park outside or in car park at rear.

Ladies: 3 from 8 different. Facilities: Jacuzzi, Sunbed & Sauna

STELLA'S ☆☆☆☆
13A, Manor St., Fenton Ratings:A-7.B- .C-6.D-7.
Open Mon-Thu + Sat/Sun 10-10.Fri. 10-12. Tel. 745490 Basic Cost £8.
Appearance: Staff young, racially varied, presentable & versatile.
Car Parking: Park around the back in Hallam St.
Ladies: 3 from 8 different Facilities: Sauna, Video & Spa Bath

STUDIO ONE ☆☆☆
531, King St., Longton Ratings:A-4.B- .C-2.D-4.
Open Mon-Sat 10-10. Sun 2-10. Tel.324191 Basic Cost £6
Appearance: Staff young, white, versatile & all shapes & sizes.
Car Parking: Very difficult here. Try around the back in Portland St.
Ladies: 2 from 9 different. Facilities:

VENUS ☆☆
230, London Rd., Stoke Ratings:A-4.B- .C-6.D-4.
Open Mon-Sat 10-10.Sun 12-9. Tel. 746060 Basic Cost £7
Appearance: Staff all ages, white, versatile & generally shapely.
Car Parking: Park across the road in Bilton St.
Ladies: 3 from 8 different. Facilities:

VOGUE ☆☆
23, Uttoxeter Rd., Longton Ratings:A-4.B- .C-9.D-4.
Open 10- 10.30 Tel. 594388 Basic Cost £5
Appearance: Staff versatile, white & all ages, shapes & sizes.
Car Parking: Park at the rear of the property.
Ladies: 2 from 6 different. Facilities:

SUFFOLK

Another predominantly rural county, but like Shropshire & Somerset we have here a county with a reasonable number of parlours. There are five in Ipswich plus one in Bury St. Edmunds.

The most unusual feature of Suffolk's parlours is that there are three in Ipswich with the same name. Normally, if an individual or company owns more than one parlour, as is often the case, they call the parlours by different names, but here alone in the country there are three Cleopatra's with the staff moving around between the three establishments. Cleopatra's 1 and 2 both have a wide range of Egyptian bits and pieces in the entrance area, lending a quaintly semi-exotic feel to both of them.

None of the six parlours have any features particularly of note, though one is not unduly pushed or hurried in any of them. Indeed, at the 3 Cleopatra's one is encouraged to have a look at the masseuses on offer at the other sister establishments, if one is disappointed by the ladies on offer at the first.

BURY ST. EDMUNDS - 01284

SOFT TOUCH ☆☆☆
89, St. John St. Ratings:A-6.B- .C-3.D-6
Open Mon- Fri 10.30-7.Sat 10.30-6. Tel.705660. Basic Cost £15.
Appearance: Staff youngish, racially varied & presentable.
Car parking: Difficult in town centre. Best bet further down the street.
Ladies:2 from 7 different. Facilities: Sauna

IPSWICH - 01473

CLEOPATRA'S ☆☆☆
6,Tacket St. Ratings:A-6.B-7.C-4.D-7.
Open Mon-Sat 10-10.30.Sun 11-10.30. Tel. 253235. Basic Cost £10.
Appearance: Staff youngish, racially varied & all shapes and sizes.
Car Parking: Difficult in Town centre, park anywhere near you can.
Ladies: 2 from 16 different. Facilities:

CLEOPATRA'S 2 ☆☆☆
15, Norwich Rd. Ratings:A-6.B-7.C-7.D-7.
Open Mon-Sat 10-10.30. Sun 11-10.30. Tel.230010. Basic Cost £10.
Appearance: Staff shared with Cleopatra's. See above.
Car Parking: Park around the back in Clarkson St.
Ladies: 2 from 16 different. Facilities: Sauna.

CLEOPATRA'S 3 ☆☆☆
9, Old Foundry Rd. Ratings:A-6.B-7.C-7.D-6.
Open Mon-Sat 10-10.30. Sun 11-10.30. Tel. 232715. Basic Cost £10.
Appearance: Staff shared with Cleopatra's. See above.
Car Parking: Park up the road.
Ladies: 2 from 16 different. Facilities:

IMAGES ☆☆☆

58, Upper Orwell St. Ratings:A-6.B-7.C-4.D-7.

Open Mon-Fri 10-10. Sat 11-7. Tel.281718. Basic Cost £12.

Appearance: Staff racially varied, all ages, shapes & sizes, including one lady who is half-Hawaiian.

Car Parking: Difficult in town centre. Park anywhere near you can.

Ladies: 2 or 3 from 12 different. Facilities:

OASIS SAUNA ☆☆☆

51, Norwich Rd. Ratings:A-7.B- .C-7.D-6.

Open Mon-Fri 10-10.Sat 10-7.Sun 11-6. Tel.259617 Basic Cost £13.

Appearance: Staff generally young. All white, some versatile. All shapes & sizes.

Car Parking: Park around the corner in Granville St.

Ladies:2 or 3 from 8 different. Facilities: Sauna & Jacuzzi

WEST MIDLANDS

The West Midlands in the heart of our country boasts a number of parlours, almost entirely located in the city of Birmingham. There are a couple to the north in Walsall & Brownhills, but even those postally listed in Warley are in truth on the western fringe of Birmingham

Birmingham is the heart of the massage industry in the West Midlands and many of the parlours have been open for many years. Manyana located just off the bottom end of the Bristol Rd. in Selly Oak has along with its neighbours, Cuddles, Regency Suite, Penny's Tonal Therapy and Good Lookers been around for many years. It features a Fantasy Room , though the features within it are somewhat limitedand it is certainly not the best equipped one I have come across.

Good Lookers and its sister establishment Burbank Massage Studio in the Edgbaston's Hagley Rd. are both long established with a range of staff of all ages and sizes.

Body Heat, run by a cheerful lady from Dublin, has a uniformly young staff of all races, but unfortunately they are not a particularly polite bunch of ladies. Ladybirds in Hockley are very friendly and eager to please as are there neighbours No. 58.

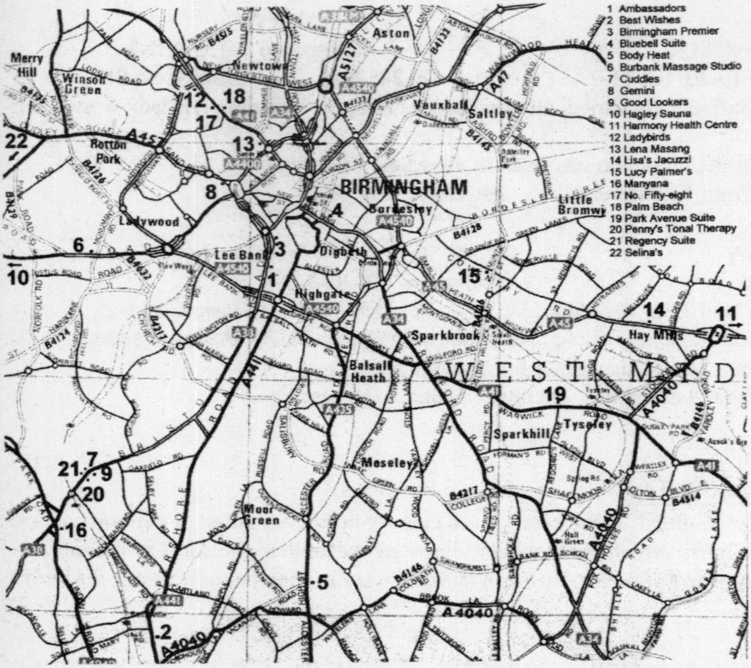

Most of the parlours are fairly ordinary. Indeed some have little to recommend them. The staff, for example, at both Digbeth's Bluebell Suite & Greet's Park Avenue Suite have certainly seen better days, though if you go for older heavily tattooed ladies, the Bluebell suite is just up your street. Cuddles is also an interesting case - and a most appropriate name - most of the ladies I have come across working there certainly are a handful and a half.

But turning to the parlours with a better star rating, three stand out. In Small Heath to the east of the city centre is Lucy Palmer's - an establishment that does not even need to advertise - it is that much of an institution. They have a first class selection of ladies, first class facilities, including sauna, jacuzzi, and videos, plus one of the most lushly decorated set of massage rooms in the country. The only off-putting feature is that getting in is almost akin to entering Fort Knox, the amount of security they use.

Left
The V.I.P. room at Lucy Palmer's

Right
A typical massage room at Lena Masang

In the city centre, literally underneath the arches in Lionel St. is Lena Masang. They have a reserved parking area, accessible through the neighbouring public car park and inside well decorated rooms and a reasonable selection of generally young attractive staff. They also have besides a jacuzzi and videos, a spa bath and steam room.

Finally not far from the original Bristol St. Motors, just off Bristol St. is Birmingham Premier. They like the above two mentioned have first class looking staff and first class facilities. Indeed they rival Lucy Palmer's.

Other parlours of note include Best Wishes, Harmony Health Centre, Palm Beach and Regency Suite. Best Wishes, newly opened in Pershore Rd., Stirchley, is tastefully decorated and with attractive staff. Harmony Health Centre in Sheldon has an attractive selection of more mature ladies in very decorous surroundings.

Palm Beach, like Lucy Palmer's feels it does not need to advertise much and you can see why - the attractiveness of the girls speaks for itself. Regency Suite has a distinctive entry area and an attractive selection of ladies to match, though the premises could perhaps do with some redecoration.

Also in Bristol Rd., which almost rivals Sheffield's Attercliffe Rd. for number of parlours, is Penny's Tonal Therapy. The staff here are generally attractive and know how to take care of their clientele.

Wolverhampton and Dudley despite their size boast no parlours and I could only find one in Coventry. With just one in Walsall and one in Willenhall, the West Midlands is another case of parlours in some localities, and hardly any elsewhere.

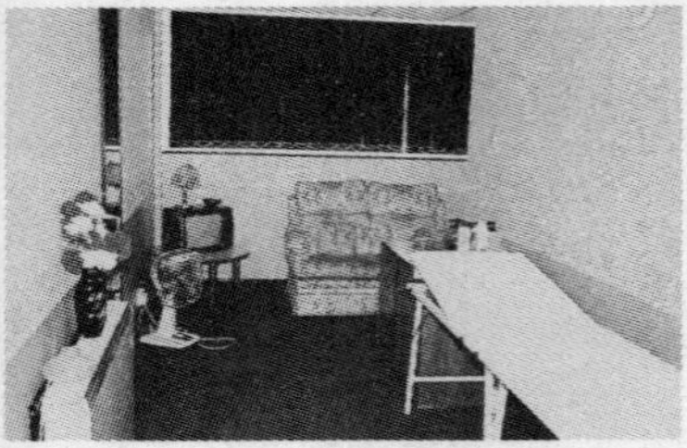

The massage room at Secrets

Outside of Birmingham the only parlour of note is right out in Brownhills. There at 139, High St. is discreetly located Secrets. The staff include some attractive ladies and the facilities, while basic are clean, tidy and well appointed.

BIRMINGHAM - 0121

AMBASSADORS ☆☆☆
92, Bristol St. Ratings:A-6.B-5.C-7.D-7.
Open:10-4.30 Tel.622 4642 Basic Cost £7.
Appearance: Staff racially varied, youngish & very versatile.
Car Parking: Park outside.
Ladies: 4 from 16 different. Facilities: Sauna, Jacuzzis, Videos & 4-Poster bed.

BEST WISHES ☆☆☆☆
1524, Pershore Rd. Ratings:A-7.B-8.C-9.D-7.
Open: Mon-Sat 10-11. Tel. 486 3860 Basic Cost £8
Appearance: Staff youngish, shapely, versatile & racially varied.
Car Parking: Drive through archway where entrance is & park at rear.
Ladies: 3 from 12 different. Facilities: Videos.

BIRMINGHAM PREMIER ☆☆☆☆☆
29, Essex St. Ratings:A-8.B- .C-6.D-7.
Open: Mon-Sat 10-4.Sun 12-4. Tel.622 6612. Basic Cost £6
Appearance: Staff young, attractive, versatile & all races, shapes & sizes.
Car Parking: Park in Essex St., using pay & display or free in Bristol St.
Ladies: 4 or 5 from 14 different. Facilities: Jacuzzi, Sunbed & Videos.

BLUEBELL SUITE ☆☆
91, Oxford St., Digbeth Ratings:A-4.B-6.C-4.D-5.
Open 10-12.30 Tel. 643 1712 Basic Cost £7
Appearance: Staff mature, generally fairly cuddly & very versatile.
Car Parking: Parking is very difficult here. Your best bets are in Oxford or Coventry St.
Ladies: 4 from 10 different. Facilities: Jacuzzi & Videos.

BODY HEAT ☆☆☆☆

3A, Kingsfield Rd., Kings Heath Ratings:A-6.B-8.C-6.D-6.

Open: Mon-Sat 10-12.Sun 11-12. Tel.441 3877 Basic Cost £8

Appearance: Staff young, racially varied & all shapes & sizes.

Car Parking: Park outside or across Alcester Rd. in Vicarage Rd.

Ladies: 3 from 6 different. Facilities: Videos.

BURBANK MASSAGE STUDIO ☆☆☆

189, Hagley Rd. Ratings:A-5.B-6.C-6.D-5.

Open: Mon-Sat 10.30-12.30 Sun.12-10. Tel. 456 4084 Basic Cost £10

Appearance: Staff versatile, all ages & racially varied. One Thai.

Car Parking: Park around the corner in Wyndham Rd.

Ladies: 3 from 10 different. Facilities: Jacuzzi, Videos & Herbal Bath.

CUDDLES ☆☆☆

629, Bristol Rd. Ratings:A-5.B-6.C-8.D-5.

Open: 11-5 Tel. 472 5261 Basic Cost £10

Appearance: Staff racially varied, versatile & all ages, shapes & sizes.

Car Parking: Park across the road in Hubert Rd.

Ladies: 3 to 6 from 20 different. Facilities: Jacuzzi & Videos.

GEMINI ☆☆☆

41B, Summer Row Ratings:A-6.B- .C-8.D-5.

Open: Mon-Fri 10-12.Sat 11-12.Sun 12-12. Tel. 236 8128. Basic Cost £10 A/V.

Appearance: Staff racially varied, versatile, young & all shapes & sizes.

Car Parking: Park off Summer Row in adjoining yard.

Ladies: 2 or 3 from 8 different. Facilities: Jacuzzi, Videos & Herbal Bath.

GOOD LOOKERS ☆☆☆

616, Bristol Rd., Selly Oak Ratings:A-6.B-5.C-7.D-5.

Open: 10-12 Tel. 471 4917 Basic Cost £8

Appearance: Staff youngish, white & versatile - all shapes & sizes.

Car Parking: Park around the corner in Tiverton Rd.

Ladies: 3 or 4 from 16 different. Facilities: Jacuzzi & Videos.

HARMONY HEALTH CENTRE ☆☆☆☆
2051, Coventry Rd., Sheldon Ratings:A-6.B-7.C-8.D-7.
Open: Mon-Fri 10-10.Sat 10.30-7. Tel. 742 6757. Basic Cost £10
Appearance: Staff mature, versatile, white, all shapes & sizes & generally attractive.
Car Parking: Park in front.
Ladies: 3 or 4 from 7 different. Facilities: Sauna, Jacuzzi & Sunbeds

LADYBIRDS ☆☆☆
Top Floor, Venture House, Hockley Hill. Ratings:A-5.B- .C-8.D-6.
Open: Mon-Sat 11-8 Tel. 507 1700 Basic Cost £8
Appearance: Staff all ages, white, petite & friendly.
Car Parking: Park in front.
Ladies: 2 from 4 different. Facilities: Videos.

LENA MASANG ☆☆☆☆☆
4B, Lionel St. Ratings:A-8.B-8.C-9.D-8.
Open: Mon-Sat 10-2.Sun 12-12. Tel. 212 9796. Basic Cost £10
Appearance: Staff young, versatile, attractive, racially varied & all shapes & sizes.
Car Parking: Park to the left at rear. Access through council car park.
Ladies: 4 from 10 different. Facilities: Jacuzzi, Videos, Spa Bath & Steam Room

LISA'S JACUZZI ☆☆☆
1160, Coventry Rd., Hay Mills Ratings: A-5.B-6.C-8.D-5.
Open: 10.30-12 Tel. 773 7837 Basic Cost £10
Appearance: Staff young, white & all shapes & sizes.
Car Parking: Park in front.
Ladies: 3 from 6 different. Facilities: Sauna, Jacuzzi & Videos.

LUCY PALMER'S ☆☆☆☆☆
399,Coventry Rd., Small Heath Ratings:A-8.B-8.C-8.D-8.
Open: Mon-Sat 10-12, Sun 12-12. Tel. 772 2417. Basic Cost £10
Appearance: Staff young, racially varied, attractive & all shapes & sizes.
Car Parking: Park in front.
Ladies: 5 from 14 different. Facilities: Sauna, Jacuzzi & Videos.

MANYANA ☆☆☆
27, Oak Tree Lane, Selly Oak Ratings:A-7.B-7.C-7.D-6.
Open: 10-12 Tel. 472 7281 Basic Cost £10.
Appearance: Staff young, racially varied & all shapes & sizes.
Car Parking: Park around the corner in Lottie Rd.
Ladies: 3 from 10 different. Facilities: Jacuzzi, Videos & Fantasy Room.

NO. FIFTY-EIGHT ☆☆☆
58, Branston St., Hockley Ratings:A-5.B- .C-8.D-5.
Open: Mon-Fri 11-11.Sat-Sun 11-10. Tel. 236 8122 Basic Cost:£8.
Appearance: Staff youngish, white, versatile & all shapes and sizes.
Car Parking: Park outside.
Ladies: 3 from 8 different. Facilities: Jacuzzi & Herbal Bath.

PALM BEACH ☆☆☆☆
4, Great Hampton St., Hockley Ratings:A-7.B- .C-5.D-6.
Open: 12-11. Tel. 236 0336 Basic Cost £10
Appearance: Staff young, attractive, racially varied & all shapes & sizes.
Car Parking: Park across the road in Hall St.
Ladies: 3 from 7 different. Facilities: Sauna & Jacuzzi.

PARK AVENUE SUITE ☆☆
572, Warwick Rd., Greet Ratings:A-4.B-4.C-8.D-4.
Open 11-6. Tel. 707 4362. Basic Cost £10
Appearance: Staff mature, white & distinctly larger than average.
Car Parking: Park outside or opposite.
Ladies: 2 ladies, always the same. Facilities: Jacuzzi.

PENNY'S TONAL THERAPY ☆☆☆☆
642, Bristol Rd., Selly Oak Ratings A-7.B-6.C-7.D-6.
Open 10-10. Tel. 472 1626 Basic Cost £10
Appearance: Staff youngish, white, versatile & all shapes & sizes.
Car Parking: Park in front or around the corner in Hubert Rd.
Ladies: 4 from 12 different. Facilities: Jacuzzi & Sunbed.

REGENCY SUITE ☆☆☆☆
631, Bristol Rd., Selly Oak Ratings:A-7.B-7.C-7.D-6.
Open Mon-Sat 10-5.Sun 12-5. Tel. 472 3668 Basic Cost £7
Appearance: Staff young, racially varied & generally slim & attractive.
Car Parking: Park across the road in Hubert Rd.
Ladies: 4 from 20 different. Facilities: Jacuzzi & Videos.

BROWNHILLS - 01543

SECRETS ☆☆☆☆
139, High St. Ratings:A-7.B-7.C-7.D-7.
Open 10-10 Tel. 454519 Basic Cost £15
Appearance: Staff youngish, slim, racially varied & versatile.
Car Parking: Park in front.
Ladies: 1 from 7 different. Facilities: Sauna & Videos.

COVENTRY - 01203

GABRIELLE'S ☆☆☆
16A, Crampers Field, Radford Ratings:A-5.B-6.C-8.D-5.
Open Mon-Fri 11-9.Sat-Sun 11-8. Tel. 594601 Basic Cost £10
Appearance: Staff cheerful, all ages, shapes & sizes, racially varied & versatile.
Car Parking: Park around the corner in Thamley Rd., where entrance is.
Ladies: 1 or 2 from 4 different. Facilities: Sauna & Videos.

WARLEY - 0121

HAGLEY SAUNA ☆☆☆
497, Hagley Rd. Ratings:A-6.B- .C-6.D-5.
Open 10.30-2 Tel. 420 2722 Basic Cost £10
Appearance: Staff young, white, shapely, friendly & versatile.
Car Parking: Park in front or around the corner in Anderson Rd.
Ladies: 2 from 8 different. Facilities: Sauna, Jacuzzi & Herbal Bath

SELINA'S ☆☆☆
350, Bearwood Rd., Bearwood Ratings: A-6.B-5.C-8.D-5.
Open Mon-Fri 10-2. Sat-Sun 10-12. Tel. 434 3845. Basic Cost £10
Appearance: Staff youngish, racially varied & versatile.
Car Parking: Park immediately outside or opposite.
Ladies: 2 or 3 from 10 different. Facilities: Jacuzzi, Videos & Fantasy Room.

WILLENHALL - 01902

ANNABEL'S SAUNA ☆☆
6, Market Place Ratings: A-5.B- .C-8.D-3.
Open Mon-Sat 10-10. Sun 12-10. Tel. 632413. Basic Cost £10.
Appearance: Staff youngish, white, slim & versatile.
Car Parking: Park in pubic car park nearby.
Ladies: 2 or 3 from 6 different. Facilities: Sauna.

WEST YORKSHIRE

Like its urban neighbours South Yorkshire and Greater Manchester, West Yorkshire has some of the most notable and most easily forgettable parlours in the whole country.

A typically luxurious massage room at Connections

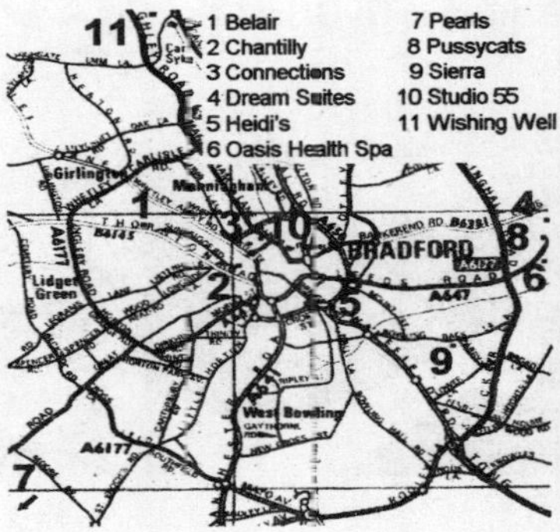

Perhaps the most notable is Connections in Bradford. It only opened early in 1996, but it is easily the most luxurious establishment in West Yorkshire, the only one in the entire area worthy of 5-star rating. The ladies working there are all attractive and the facilities are excellent. The only puzzling feature of it is how the place is not that busy. Every time I have been there the ladies are sitting around with no clients in sight. Maybe I have just turned up at the wrong time, maybe it is its location, situated above a notable Indian restaurant in the city centre. Certainly the location might be deemed more suitable for other more conventional activities, a casino perhaps, but I feel confident that in time, the advantages of convenient parking as well as first class staff and facilities will become realised by those wanting a massage in West Yorkshire and then business will perk up there.

In the Leeds Rd, Thornbury is Oasis Health Spa, located in small premises but where a number of exceptionally attractive ladies work. Also of note in Bradford are

Chantilly, Dream Suites & Studio 55. Chantilly, unfortunately located several floors up in an old mill is tiring to get to but with an attractive range of ladies to pick from, once you get up there. Dream Suites has a fine range of facilities, with a well equipped stoneroom as well as the more usual sauna, jacuzzi, videos etc. Studio 55 is clean, tidy and boasts attractive youngish staff.

In Leeds there are a number of well appointed parlours with reasonably good looking staff - in the city centre Mayfair and Ladybirds, in Kirkstall Delilah's Health Studio, in Holbeck Hi-Q Sauna and in Harehills Elite Sauna. The best in Leeds is probably Hi-Q Sauna, tastefully decorated and with friendly and not unattractive staff. Also note should be made of Zenith in Woodhouse, where there is a particularly attractive Norwegian lady working.

The V.I.P. room at Hi-Q Sauna

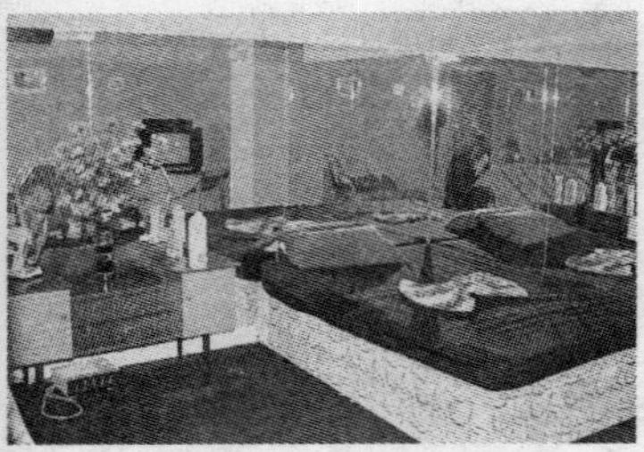

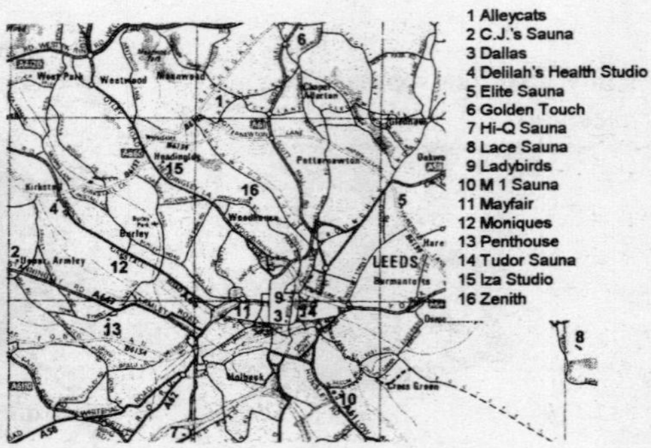

Note also must be made of the situation in Dewsbury. This town boasts two parlours - Sunshine Supertan and Sunspot Sauna - similar names but very different establishments. Suffice it to say that Sunspot Sauna is probably the least attractive in West Yorkshire and it is not even that easy to park near! Sunshine Supertan, on the other hand, is a delight. Curiously located in a block of offices opposite the railway station, with accountants and solicitors nearby, the place is cleanly and tidily run with a very pleasant bunch of ladies in attendance. The proprietress is a charming lady who is now considering using the premises as a mixed sauna club for certain nights in the week. Before turning up it might be an idea to see how far this idea has progressed.

Finally there is an interesting parlour in Ossett, just to the west of Wakefield. Located in an industrial unit is Springfield Sauna. The establishment boasts a sauna & a reasonably equipped fantasy room. The girls are racially varied including a sultry, fiery young lady of mixed German & Irish parentage, which no doubt accounts for her nature.

Left
The unusual L-shaped massage room at Sunshine Supertan

Right
The V.I.P. room at Springfield Sauna

BRADFORD - 01274

BEL AIR ☆☆☆
338, Thornton Rd. Ratings: A-6.B- .C-9.D-7.
Open: Sat-Wed 11-10. Thurs-Fri 11-4 Tel. 488410. Basic Cost £6
Appearance: Staff slim, racially varied, youngish & versatile.
Car Parking: Park off the road in front.
Ladies: 2 from 11 different. Facilities: Fantasy Room, Jacuzzi & Videos.

CHANTILLY ☆☆☆☆
11, Fulton St. Ratings: A-7.B- .C-5.D-6.
Open: 10-9. Tel. 741885. Basic Cost: £6
Appearance: Staff youngish, white & versatile. Mainly slim including one half-Italian.
Car Parking: Park around the corner in Sunbridge Rd.
Ladies: 2 to 4 from 7 different. Facilities: Sauna, Jacuzzi & Videos.

CONNECTIONS ☆☆☆☆☆
Above The Bombay Brasserie, Simes St. Ratings: A-8.B- .C-9.D-8.
Open: Mon-Fri 10.30 - 10.Sat-Sun 11-9.Tel. 743432. Basic Cost: £6
Appearance: Staff young, racially varied, slimmish, friendly & all very attractive.
Car Parking: Park in Brasserie Car Park off Rawson Rd.
Ladies: 4 from 10 different. Facilities: Sauna, Jacuzzi & Video.

DREAM SUITES ☆☆☆☆
979-981, Leeds Rd., Thornbury Ratings:A-6.B-6 C-10.D-5.
Open: 10 - 4.30. Tel. 666926 Basic Cost £5
Appearance: Staff are young, versatile, racially varied & all shapes and sizes.
Car Parking: Drive in through gates & park securely on premises.
Ladies: 2 to 6 from 18 different. Facilities: Sauna, Jacuzzi, Videos, Spa Bath, Sunbeds & Stoneroom.

HEIDI'S ☆☆☆
1, Downham St. Ratings:A-6.B- .C-9.D-6.
Open Sat-Wed 10-10. Thurs-Fri 10-4. Tel. 743612. Basic Cost £6.
Appearance: Staff youngish, friendly, racially varied & versatile.
Car Parking: Park opposite.
Ladies: 3 from 17 different. Facilities: Sauna & Videos.

OASIS HEALTH SPA ☆☆☆☆
1270, Leeds Rd., Thornbury Ratings:A-7.B- .C-8.D-5.
Open: Mon-Sat 10-10.Sun 11-10. Tel.663148. Basic Cost: £7.
Appearance: Staff young & racially varied including some great lookers.
Car Parking: Park outside or opposite.
Ladies: 2 from 8 different. Facilities: Sauna & Videos.

PEARLS ☆☆
4, Mount Pleasant St., Queensbury. Ratings:A-4.B- .C-8.D-6.
Open: Mon-Fri 10-9. Sat 10-6. Tel. 880331. Basic Cost: £6
Appearance: Staff mature, white, versatile & all shapes & sizes.
Car Parking: Park outside or in High St. around the corner.
Ladies: 2 or 3 from 6 different. Facilities: Sauna, Jacuzzi & Videos.

PUSSYCATS ☆☆☆
Unit 10, 935, Leeds Rd., Thornbury. Ratings: A-5.B-5.C-9.D-6.
Open: 10-4. Tel. 668502. Basic Cost £5
Appearance: Staff youngish, shapely, white & versatile.
Car Parking: At rear of industrial estate. Park by building.
Ladies: 2 or 3 from 6 different. Facilities: Sauna & Videos.

SIERRA ☆☆☆
1, Lesarna Ct., Bowling Back Lane. Ratings: A-5.B-5.C-9.D-6.
Open: 10.30-10 Tel. 722945. Basic Cost £6.
Appearance: Staff young, white, versatile & all shapes & sizes.
Car Parking: On Industrial estate. Park by building.
Ladies: 2 from 6 different. Facilities: Sauna, Jacuzzi & Videos.

STUDIO 55 ☆☆☆☆
55, North Parade. Ratings: A-7.B-6.C-5.D-7.
Open: Mon-Sat 10.30-10.30. Sun 11-10. Tel. 736874. Basic Cost £8.
Appearance: Staff youngish, racially varied & attractive.
Car Parking: Difficult in city centre. Ideally use Rawson Rd.
Ladies: 2 from 8 different. Facilities: Sauna & Videos.

WISHING WELL ☆☆☆
263, Bradford Rd., Frizinghall Ratings: A-6.B- C-7.D-7.
Open: Mon-Sat 10-10. Tel. 490803 Basic Cost £8
Appearance: Staff all ages, presentable, racially varied & versatile.
Car Parking: Single yellow line outside. Park further down the road.
Ladies: 2 to 4 from 12 different. Facilities: Sauna & Jacuzzi.

DEWSBURY - 01924

SUNSHINE SUPERTAN ☆☆☆☆
15, Wellington Rd. Ratings: A-7.B- .C-8.D-6.
Open: Mon-Fri 10-9. Sat-Sun 10-8. Tel.452279. Basic Cost £8.
Appearance: Staff racially varied, youngish & presentable. One Brazilian.
Car Parking: Use Station Car Park opposite.
Ladies: 3 from 9 different. Facilities: Sauna, Videos & Amusement machine.

SUNSPOT SAUNA ☆
2A, Market St. Ratings: A-3.B- .C-2.D-3.
Open: Mon-Fri 10-10. Sat-Sun 11-9. Tel. 461483. Basic Cost £6.
Appearance: Staff young, white, cheerful & versatile.
Car Parking: Parking very difficult in town centre. Park anywhere you can.
Ladies: 4 from 9 different. Facilities: Sauna & Jacuzzi.

ILKLEY - 01943

FOUNTAIN HEALTH & BEAUTY SALON ☆☆☆
2A, Station Rd., Burley-in-Wharfdale. Ratings: A-5.B- .C-8.D-7.
Open: Mon-Fri 11-9. Sat-Sun 12-6. Tel. 863630. Basic Cost £5.
Appearance: Staff white, youngish, versatile & all shapes and sizes.
Car Parking: Park outside or further up Station Rd.
Ladies: 2 or 3 from 8 different. Facilities: Sauna.

LEEDS - 0113

ALLEYCATS ☆☆☆
8A, Stonegate Rd. Ratings: A-6.B- .C-7.D-5.
Open: Mon-Fri 10-10.Sat-Sun 10-8.30. Tel. 230 4864. Basic Cost £5.
Appearance: Staff youngish, white, versatile & all shapes and sizes.
Car Parking: Park around the corner in Stainbeck Ave.
Ladies: 2 from 8 different. Facilities: 4-Poster Bed & Videos.

C.J.'s SAUNA ☆☆
134, Stanningley Rd. Ratings:A-5.B- .C-8.D-5.
Open: 10-10. Tel. 263 5718 Basic Cost £5
Appearance: Staff young, racially varied, versatile & all shapes and sizes.
Car Parking: Park in front or around the corner in Wyther Park St.
Ladies: 2 or 3 from 6 different. Facilities: Sauna.

DALLAS ☆☆☆
168, Lower Briggate Ratings:A-5.B- .C-3.D-5.
Open Mon-Fri 10-12. Sat 10-10. Sun 12-10. Tel. 245 0833. Basic Cost £8
Appearance: Staff youngish, presentable, racially varied & versatile.
Car Parking: In city centre. Park nearby using pay & display.
Ladies: 2 or 3 from 7 different. Facilities: Sauna.

DELILAH'S HEALTH STUDIO ☆☆☆☆
12, Commercial Rd., Kirkstall Ratings:A-8.B-6.C-7.D-7.
Open 10-11. Tel. 230 7557. Basic Cost £10.
Appearance: Staff young, racially varied, versatile & attractive.
Car Parking: Park 50 yards down the road.
Ladies: 3 from 12 different. Facilities: Sauna, Videos & Electronic Bed.

ELITE SAUNA ☆☆☆☆
225, Harehills Lane Ratings:A-7.B- .C-7.D-7.
Open: 10-9. Tel. 235 9033. Basic Cost £6.
Appearance: Staff racially varied, versatile & all shapes & sizes, including one Italian lady.
Car Parking: Park around the corner in Dorset Terrace.
Ladies: 3 from 9 different. Facilities: Sauna & Videos.

GOLDEN TOUCH ☆☆☆
10, Whinbrook Cres. Ratings:A-5.B- .C-8.D-4.
Open: Mon-Fri 10.30-10.Sat-Sun 12-9. Tel. 268 8688. Basic Cost £6.
Appearance: Staff white, mature & all shapes and sizes.
Car Parking: Park in front.
Ladies: 2 from 6 different. Facilities: Videos.

HI-Q SAUNA ☆☆☆☆
78, Elland Rd. Ratings: A-7.B- .C-7.D-7.
Open: Mon-Sat 11-9.Sun 1-9. Tel. 277 2769. Basic Cost £5.
Appearance: Staff young, mainly slim & racially varied.
Car Parking: In awkward to get at area by M621. Park outside.
Ladies: 3 from 10 different. Facilities: Sauna, Videos, Sunbed & Gym

LACE SAUNA ☆☆☆
6A, Barleyhill Rd., Garforth Ratings: A-6.B- .C-9.D-5.
Open: Mon-Fri 11-8.30. Sat 11-7.30. Tel. 287 3124. Basic Cost £6.
Appearance: Staff young, slim & versatile.
Car Parking: Use free public car park next door.
Ladies: 2 from 4 different. Facilities: Sauna.

LADYBIRDS ☆☆☆☆
20, Albion Place Ratings: A-7.B- .C-1.D-7.
Open: Mon-Sat 10-9. Tel. 234 3964 Basic Cost £5
Appearance: Staff white, mature, versatile & all shapes & sizes.
Car Parking: Very difficult in city centre. Find a space anywhere.
Ladies: 3 from 5 different. Facilities: Sauna

M1 SAUNA ☆☆☆
207, Hunslet Rd. Ratings: A-6.B-5.C-9.D-5.
Open: 11-1. Tel. 245 5700 Basic Cost £5
Appearance: Staff youngish, mainly slim, versatile & racially varied, inc.one Filipino.
Car Parking: Turn into Pym St. & park around the back.
Ladies: 2 from 10 different. Facilities: Sauna & Videos.

MAYFAIR ☆☆☆☆
24A, York Place Ratings: A-7.B-7.C-5.D-6.
Open: 11-11.30 Tel. 244 8381. Basic Cost £6.
Appearance: Staff youngish, racially varied & versatile.
Car Parking: Park outside on a meter.
Ladies: 2 from 9 different. Facilities: Sauna, Jacuzzi & Videos.

MONIQUES ☆☆☆
331, Kirkstall Rd. Ratings: A-6.B- .C-7.D-5.
Open: 24 hours a day Tel. 263 5462. Basic Cost £5.
Appearance: Staff youngish, racially varied & versatile. One Chinese.
Car Parking: Park across the road in Haddon Rd.
Ladies: 3 from 12 different. Facilities: Sauna & Videos.

PENTHOUSE ☆☆
18A, Town St., Armley Ratings: A-4.B- .C-6.D-3.
Open: 10-10. Tel. 263 7598 Basic Cost £5.
Appearance: Staff all ages, races, shapes & sizes.
Car Parking: Park over the road & around the corner in Wesley Rd.
Ladies: 2 from 6 different. Facilities: Sauna, Videos & 4-Poster Bed.

TUDOR SAUNA ☆☆☆
96, Kirkgate Ratings: A-5.B- .C-3.D-6.
Open: 10-9. Tel. 245 0348 Basic Cost £6
Appearance: Staff white, mature, presentable & versatile.
Car Parking: In city centre - use any pay & display you can find.
Ladies: 3 from 9 different. Facilities: Sauna.

12A STUDIO ☆☆
12A, Otley Rd. Ratings: A-3.B- .C-8.D-4.
Open: Mon-Fri 10.30-10.Sat-Sun 10.30-8.30. Tel. 230 6059. Basic Cost £6.
Appearance: Staff white, versatile & all ages, shapes & sizes.
Car Parking: Park around the back in Shire Oak St. - entry at rear up fire escape.
Ladies: 3 from 5 different. Facilities:

ZENITH ☆☆☆☆
4, Christopher Rd. Ratings: A-7.B- .C-7.D-6.
Open: Mon-Fri 10-10. Sat-Sun 10-8. Tel. 244 5446. Basic Cost £5.
Appearance: Staff youngish & shapely. One Norwegian.
Car Parking: Park outside or opposite.
Ladies: 2 from 7 different. Facilities: Sauna & Videos.

OSSETT - 01924

SPRINGFIELD SAUNA ☆☆☆☆
Unit 9, Springfield Mills, Spring End Rd. Ratings:A-7.B- .C-9.D-7.
Open: 11-2. Tel. 263030. Basic Cost £10.
Appearance: Staff racially varied, versatile, attractive & mainly young. One lady is half-German, half-Irish.
Car Parking: On industrial estate. Park outside.
Ladies: 2 or 3 from 10 different. Facilities: Sauna, Videos & Fantasy Room.

WAKEFIELD - 01924

A KIND OF MAGIC ☆☆
Unit 4, Church St. Ratings:A-4.B- .C-9.D-4.
Open: 10.30-7. Tel. 291852. Basic Cost: £5.
Appearance: Staff young, white & versatile.
Car Parking: On industrial estate. Park by the unit.
Ladies: 2 from 8 different. Facilities: Videos.

WILTSHIRE

Another predominantly rural county, with again only a handful of parlours. One in Swindon & two, curiously, in the small town of Chippenham.

Unfortunately I have not been able to look over Wiltshire's three parlours in any great detail but two I feel show potential. In particular St. Tropez in Swindon has a competent attractive manageress by the name of Zoe with staff to match, though only limited facilities.

Dallas Health Studio in Chippenham has a wide range of facilities and a pleasing decor. The staff are friendly with two ladies from Southern Europe, a recent arrival being Amanda who used to run Bath Road Massage in Bristol with such gusto. There is also convenient parking at the rear of the premises in Dallas Rd.

CHIPPENHAM - 01249

DALLAS HEALTH STUDIO ☆☆☆☆
93, Marshfield Rd. Ratings:A-7.B- .C-9.D-6.
Open: Mon-Sat 11-10. Sun 12-9. Tel. 448240. Basic Cost £10.
Appearance: Staff young, presentable, racially varied & versatile, including ladies from Italy & Greece.
Car Parking: Park at rear of premises off Dallas Rd.
Ladies: 2 or 3 from 8 different. Facilities: Sauna, Jacuzzi, Videos & Waterbed.

LA FEMME ☆☆☆
5, Langley Rd. Ratings:A-5.B- .C-7.D-5.
Open: Mon-Fri 11-9.30.Sat 11-8.30. Sun 12-6. Tel. 444251. Basic Cost:
Appearance: Staff young & presentable.
Car Parking: Park outside or in neighbouring Hathaway Retail Park.
Ladies: 2 from 8 different. Facilities: Jacuzzi & Videos.

SWINDON - 01793

ST. TROPEZ ☆☆☆☆
137, Victoria Rd. Ratings:A-7.B- .C-4.D-5.
Open: 10-12. Tel. 495905.Basic Cost: £20.
Appearance: Staff racially varied, young & versatile, including ladies from Sweden & Italy.
Car Parking: Park around the corner in King John St. or use pay & display in Prospect Place.
Ladies: 4 from 20 different. Facilities: Videos.

Part 2. Scotland

CENTRAL

Central region is the only part of Scotland other than the two major cities - Edinburgh & Glasgow to have any parlours. Not that it boasts many - there is only one in the principle town of Falkirk. It is however, apparently a very busy parlour. This cannot be due to its staff, decor or facilities, since none of these features, while perfectly acceptable, are anything out of the ordinary.

FALKIRK - 01324

BUBBLES HEALTH SPA ☆☆☆
232, Graham Rd. Ratings:A-5.B- .C-8.D-5.
Open: Mon-Sat 11.30-9.30. Sun 12-6. Tel. 620175. Basic Cost £10.
Appearance: Staff young, white & all shapes and sizes.
Car Parking: Park outside.
Ladies: 3 from 12 different. Facilities: Jacuzzi & Videos.

LOTHIAN

Lothian district or so far as anyone wanting massage is concerned, Edinburgh boasts some of the best parlours in the entire country. Uniquely for any area in the country, the parlours here seem to be much more conservative when it comes to their names. None had changed their name between producing the first and now this guide. That does not mean that the establishments are conservative when it comes to the staff, decor and facilities. Some of the parlours here are not to be outdone anywhere else in the United Kingdom.

Without a doubt the top 4 parlours are Blair Street Sauna, London Street Sauna, Penthouse & Scorpio. Blair Street in the Old Town is a tastefully decorated establishment with 5 or 6 ladies there at any time, totally mirrored rooms plus first class facilities.

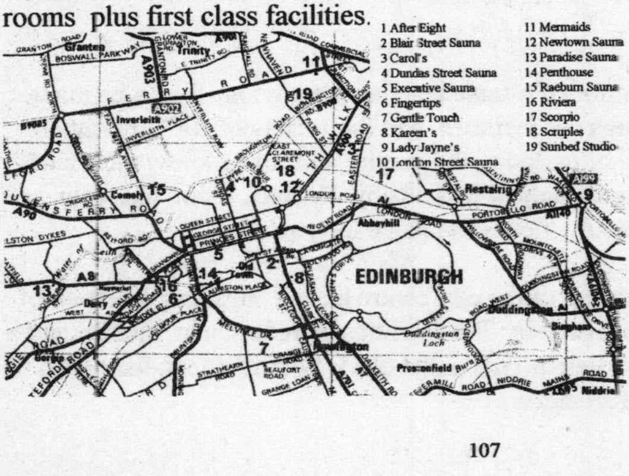

London Street goes two or three stages further with ultra violet light in the rooms to highlight the charms of the masseuses plus full air conditioning. Unique among the parlours I have visited, one is greeted not only by 6 or 7 lovely ladies, but a parrot as well. Who's a pretty boy then??

Two of the ladies plus the parrot from London Street Sauna

A typically luxurious massage room at London Street Sauna

Rivalling London Street are two more parlours - Penthouse also located in the centre and Scorpio, located just around the corner from Hibernian's football ground at Easter Rd. Penthouse could well be the most luxuriously decorated establishment in the country, with between 6 and 9 ladies there at any time and amongst the facilities on offer a waterbed as well as the totally mirrored rooms, sauna, steam room, jacuzzi etc. one finds in all the best Scottish establishments.

Left
The entrance lobby at Penthouse

Right
A typical compact luxury massage room at Newtown Sauna

Scorpio is a little more basic but having enjoyed a massage there myself, I can attest personally to the quality of the ladies working there. The establishment is tastefully decorated and features totally mirrored rooms, sauna, jacuzzis etc.

Also of note is Newtown Sauna; the rooms are compact and lack jacuzzis, but the establishment is clean, tidy, pleasantly decorated and the ladies are all young and attractive.

Besides the above mentioned establishments, mention must also be made of Mermaids in Leith. Although the facilities and the variety of staff are rather more limited than at many other parlours, the mature staff there know their work and enjoy it. Run by an engaging lady, a Miss Ruby Thomas, if you like your massage from a more mature lady, this is the place for you.

Paradise Sauna, to the west of the city centre has an engaging selection of young ladies and friendly management. The facilities include sauna, jacuzzi and a steam room. The staff who include a Thai and a black South African lady, also include several capable Scottish ladies.

Riviera, a little nearer the city centre is not as pleasantly decorated, but the ladies are just as lovely and the establishment features a totally mirrored room .

But Edinburgh also has its share of less distinguished parlours. Fingertips besides being awkward to park near struck me as a rather tawdry parlour ,despite the fact that it advertises as aggressively as any of the many other parlours in the city. I will keep my eye on it.

If your taste is to the more unusual type of massage, Kareen's, several floors up in Nicholson St. may be just up your street. The staff are not unattractive and engagingly versatile.

EDINBURGH - 0131

AFTER EIGHT ☆☆☆
8, Spittal St. Ratings: A-6.B- .C-4.D-5.
Open Mon-Sat 12-8. Tel. 221 0872. Basic Cost £10.
Appearance: Staff white, versatile and all ages.
Car Parking: Difficult so near the city centre. Try & find a free meter.
Ladies: 2 from 6 different. Facilities: Videos.

BLAIR STREET SAUNA ☆☆☆☆
30, Blair St. Ratings: A-8.B- .C-4.D-8.
Open: Mon-Sat 10-10.Sun 1-10. Tel. 226 2114. Basic Cost £12.
Appearance: Staff young & racially varied. One Spanish.
Car Parking: Park outside or opposite using pay & display.
Ladies: 5 or 6 from 13 different. Facilities: Sauna, Videos & Totally mirrored rooms.

CAROL'S ☆☆☆
320, Easter Rd. Ratings: A-5.B- .C-8.D-5.
Open: 10-10. Tel. 554 0109. Basic Cost £10
Appearance: Staff white, versatile & all ages, shapes & sizes.
Car Parking: Park opposite or just down the road.
Ladies: 4 or 5 from 10 different. Facilities: Videos.

DUNDAS STREET SAUNA ☆☆☆
168, Dundas St. Ratings: A-5.B- .C-4.D-6.
Open Mon-Sat 10-10. Sun 1-10. Tel. 558 1564. Basic Cost £15.
Appearance: Staff young, racially varied & all shapes & sizes.
Car Parking: In a residents permit holders only area. Find a meter nearby.
Ladies: 5 or 6 from 15 different. Facilities: Sauna & Videos.

EXECUTIVE SAUNA ☆☆☆
87/89, Rose Lane North Ratings: A-5.B- .C-3.D-6.
Open 10.30-10.45. Tel. 225 5242. Basic Cost £11.
Appearance: Staff young, presentable & versatile. One Polynesian.
Car Parking: In city centre - use pay & display in Charlotte Square or Queen St.
Ladies: 4 from 20 different. Facilities: Sauna & Jacuzzi.

FINGERTIPS ☆
209, Fountainbridge Ratings: A-4.B-5.C-2.D-4.
Open 11-11. Tel. 229 9888. Basic Cost £10 A/V.
Appearance: Staff mature, white, versatile & all shapes & sizes.
Car Parking: Parking locally very difficult. Best bet locally is Grove St.
Ladies: 3 from 10 different. Facilities:

GENTLE TOUCH ☆☆☆
40, Argyle Pl. Ratings: A-6.B- .C-4.D-5.
Open: Sun-Fri 11-11. Tel. 229 7782. Basic Cost £10.
Appearance: Staff youngish, white, versatile & all shapes & sizes. One German.
Car Parking: Use pay & display opposite.
Ladies: 2 from 6 different. Facilities: Videos.

KAREEN'S ☆☆☆
18, Nicholson St. Ratings:A-7.B- .C-4.D-7.
Open: 11- 9.30 Tel. 667 2255. Basic Cost £10.
Appearance: Staff youngish, personable & very versatile
Car Parking: Park anywhere near using pay & display.
Ladies: 1 from 4 different. Facilities: Videos & Fantasy Room.

LADY JAYNE'S ☆☆☆
9, Seafield Rd. East Ratings: A-5.B- .C-9.D-5.
Open: Mon-Sat 11-10. Sun 1-10. Tel. 657 5257. Basic Cost £10 A/V.
Appearance: Staff youngish, white & versatile.
Car Parking: Park in front.
Ladies: 2 or 3 from 5 different. Facilities: Videos.

LONDON STREET SAUNA ☆☆☆☆☆

41, London St. Ratings: A-8.B- .C-5.D-9.

Open: Mon-Sat 10.30-10. Sun 2-10. Tel. 556 8848. Basic Cost £12.

Appearance: Staff racially varied, friendly, cheerful & attractive including ladies from Greece, Thailand, Sweden & Brazil.

Car Parking: Park opposite using pay & display.

Ladies: 6 or 7 from 24 different. Facilities: Totally mirrored rooms, Sauna, Steam Room, Jacuzzi, Videos, Ultra-violet lighting & Air conditioning

MERMAIDS ☆☆☆☆

13, Ferry Rd. Ratings: A-6.B- .C-6.D-5.

Open: Mon-Fri 11.30-10. Sat-Sun 12-10. Tel. 553 4688. Basic Cost £15.

Appearance: Staff versatile, white, mature, presentable & friendly.

Car Parking: Park opposite by Leith Public Library.

Ladies: 2 from 5 different. Facilities: Videos & Sunbed.

NEWTOWN SAUNA ☆☆☆☆

17B, Hart St. Ratings: A-7.B- .C-4.D-7.

Open: Mon-Sat 10-10. Sun 1-10. Tel. 557 3616. Basic Cost £15.

Appearance: Staff all ages, some slim, some shapely, racially varied & attractive.

Car Parking: In a resident permit holders only area. Find a meter nearby.

Ladies: 3 to 6 from 10 different. Facilities: Sauna & Videos.

PARADISE SAUNA ☆☆☆☆

55, Roseburn Terrace Ratings: A-6.B- .C-7.D-6.

Open: Mon-Sat 11-11. Sun 12-10. Tel. 346 8717. Basic Cost £15.

Appearance: Staff young, mainly slim & versatile, inc. a Thai & a black South African.

Car Parking: Park around the corner in Roseburn Cres.

Ladies: 4 or 5 from 12 different. Facilities: Sauna, Jacuzzi, Videos & Steam Room.

PENTHOUSE ☆☆☆☆☆

91, Lothian Rd. Ratings: A-7.B- .C-4.D-9.

Open: 11-12. Tel. 229 3260. Basic Cost £15.

Appearance: Staff racially varied, versatile, mostly young & attractive, inc. 2 Brazilians & a Thai.

Car Parking: Find & use a meter in Grindlay St. After 5.30 use Grindlay St. Court.

Ladies: 6 to 9 from 20 different. Facilities: Sauna, Jacuzzi, Videos, Waterbed & Totally Mirrored rooms.

RAEBURN SAUNA ☆☆
43, Comely Bank Rd. Ratings: A-5.B- .C-5.D-4.
Open: Mon-Sat 11-10.Sun 2-10. Tel. 332 3247. Basic Cost £12.
Appearance: Staff youngish, white & presentable.
Car Parking: Park outside or across the road.
Ladies: 3 from 4 different. Facilities:

RIVIERA ☆☆☆☆
12-14, Torpichen Place Ratings: A-7.B-5.C-5.D-6.
Open: Mon-Sat 11-11. Sun 1-11. Tel. 229 9312. Basic Cost £15.
Appearance: Staff young, white & mainly slim.
Car Parking: Difficult - try & find a meter off Palmerston Pl.
Ladies: 3 from 7 different. Facilities: Sauna, Jacuzzi, Videos & Totally Mirrored Room.

SCORPIO ☆☆☆☆☆
42, Albion Rd. Ratings: A-8.B-9.C-9.D-8.
Open: Mon-Sat 10-10. Sun 1-10. Tel. 661 9944. Basic Cost £15.
Appearance: Staff young, racially varied & attractive. One Thai, one Sudanese.
Car Parking: Park outside or opposite.
Ladies: 7 from 30 different. Facilities: Sauna, Jacuzzi, Videos & Totally Mirrored Rooms.

SCRUPLES ☆☆☆
28, West Annandale St. Ratings: A-6.B- .C-5.D-4.
Open: Mon-Sat 11-11.Sun 1-11.Tel. 557 8742. Basic Cost £10.
Appearance: Staff young, racially varied & versatile.
Car Parking: Difficult. Ideally park outside or across the street.
Ladies: 2 from 20 different. Facilities: Sauna & Videos.

SUNBED STUDIO ☆☆☆
278, Bonnington Rd. Ratings: A-7.B- .C-8.D-4.
Open: Mon-Sat 11-10. Tel. 554 2455. Basic Cost £10.
Appearance: Staff white, cheerful, versatile & all ages.
Car Parking: Park up the road on same or opposite side.
Ladies: 4 from 10 different. Facilities: Sunbed.

STRATHCLYDE

Strathclyde essentially, so far as massage is concerned, means Glasgow and Glasgow boasts a first class selection of parlours, amongst which three particularly stand out. The two top quality establishments are the Carlton Club and Parkgrove House. The Carlton Club, located quietly in an office area overlooking the Clyde has only a limited range of ladies, though all are attractive, but a first class range of facilities, second to none in the whole country. Their totally mirrored rooms also include large circular beds and en-suite jacuzzis, especially for the disabled.

Parkgrove House, located on the edge of Kelvingrove park, has almost as large a range of facilities, but a choice of even more ladies with 7 there at all times from a range of 32 different, including ladies of all races, generally young and attractive.

Left
Parkgrove House

Right
A massage room
at Parkgrove

Bubbles Health Studio in Merrylee on the southern fringe of the city has convenient on site parking and a pleasant-looking range of staff. The St. Enoch Club, located in a top floor site has an attractive waiting lounge and a young exuberant selection of ladies, though the other facilities are somewhat limited. Apparently some of the staff are amenable to more unusual massage requests.

On the edge of Kelvingrove Park is a delightful parlour. Woodlands Health Salon has very attractive staff, although the facilities are somewhat limited. One lady in particular, I found very friendly and amenable, apparently part-Malay, her

Scottish accent seemed somewhat out of place,though her smile and pleasant manner were all one could have hoped for.

Finally mention must be made of Tropical Palms. Sited in the city centre not far from Glasgow's main police station, Archie McCracken runs an enterprising operation. Fantasies of all kinds can be arranged, the staff there besides being mainly young and attractive are also extremely versatile. Furthermore all credit cards are accepted there.

GLASGOW - 0141

AQUARIUS SAUNA ☆☆☆
6, Park Quadrant Ratings:A-6.B- .C-4.D-7.
Open: Mon-Sat 11-12. Sun 2-12. Tel. 332 9344. Basic Cost £15 Appearance: Staff young, cheerful, racially varied & shapely, inc. two Thais & one Australian.
Car Parking: Plenty of free spaces around if you can find one vacant.
Ladies: 5 or 6 from 20 different. Facilities: Sauna, Jacuzzi, Videos, Pool Room & Steam Room.

BUBBLES HEALTH STUDIO ☆☆☆☆
4, Fenwick Rd., Merrylee Ratings: A-6.B- .C-9.D-7.
Open: Mon-Fri 10-10. Sat 11.30-9. Tel. 633 1002. Basic Cost £14.
Appearance: Staff youngish, white & all shapes & sizes.
Car Parking: Park on premises off Merrylee Cres.
Ladies: 3 from 7 different. Facilities: Sauna & Jacuzzi.

CARLTON CLUB ☆☆☆☆☆
42, Carlton Place Ratings: A-8.B- .C-7.D-9.
Open: 11-12. Tel. 429 4202. Basic Cost: £15 A/V/AE.
Appearance: Staff young, shapely, attractive & racially varied, inc. one Venezuelan.
Car Parking: Park outside, spaces generally available.
Ladies: 4 from 10 different. Facilities: Sauna, Jacuzzis, Videos, Large circular beds, Totally mirrored rooms & Sunbeds.

EXPRESSIONS SALON ☆☆☆
198, Battlefield Rd. Ratings: A-6.B- .C-7.D-6.
Open: Mon-Sat 11-10. Sun 11-6. Tel. 649 5792. Basic Cost £10.
Appearance: Staff white, Scottish, youngish & versatile.
Car Parking: Park outside or across the street.
Ladies: 1 from 5 different. Facilities: Videos.

FEMMES ☆☆☆
520, Victoria Rd. Ratings: A-5.B- .C-6 D-5.
Open: 10-11. Tel. 423 7424. Basic Cost: £10.
Appearance: Staff white, young & all shapes & sizes.
Car Parking: Park around the corner in Albert Ave.
Ladies: 1 from 6 different. Facilities: Videos.

HYDE PARK AROMATHERAPY ☆☆
150, Hyde Park St. Ratings: A-4.B- .C-10.D-5.
Open: 10.30-10.30 Tel. 221 5991 Basic Cost: £10.
Appearance: Staff Scottish, racially varied, versatile & all ages, shapes & sizes.
Car Parking: Park on premises.
Ladies: 4 from 17 different. Facilities: Videos.

NEW BLYTHSWOOD HEALTH CLUB ☆☆☆
41B, York St. Ratings: A-6.B- .C-5 D-6.
Open:11-11. Tel. 204 3434 Basic Cost:£10.
Appearance: Staff young, white & all shapes and sizes.
Car Parking: Park opposite.
Ladies: 3 from 7 different. Facilities: Sauna, Videos & Steam Room.

NEW EXECUTIVE CLUB ☆☆☆
20, Brunswick St. Ratings: A-5.B- .C-6 D-5.
Open: Mon-Sat 10-10. Sun 12-8.Tel. 552 1181. Basic Cost £10.
Appearance: Staff racially varied and all ages, shapes and sizes.
Car Parking: Park up the street.
Ladies: 2 from 6 different. Facilities: Sauna, Sunbed & Videos.

OASIS HEALTH CLUB ☆☆☆
3, Bath St. Ratings: A-6.B- .C-4 D-7.
Open: 11-11. Tel. 332 6092. Basic Cost £10 A/V.
Appearance: Staff all Scottish, white & versatile.
Car Parking: Park on a meter nearby.
Ladies: 3 from 15 different. Facilities: Sauna, Videos & Steam Room.

PARKGROVE HOUSE ☆☆☆☆☆
1, Parkgrove Terrace Ratings: A-9.B- .C-7 D-8.
Open: Mon-Fri 11-1. Sat-Sun 11-12. Tel. 334 6006. Basic Cost £15.
Appearance: Staff young, attractive and racially varied One Australian.
Car Parking: Park outside. Entrance is in Derby St.
Ladies: 7 from 32 different. Facilities: Sauna, Jacuzzis, Sunbed, Steam Room & Videos.

ST. ENOCH CLUB ☆☆☆☆
56, Howard St. Ratings: A-7.B- .C-6.D-7.
Open: 11-11. Tel. 226 5258. Basic Cost £8 A/V.
Appearance: Staff racially varied, versatile & all ages, shapes and sizes.
Car Parking: Park in front.
Ladies: 4 from 20 different. Facilities: Videos.

TROPICAL PALMS ☆☆☆☆
138, Holland St. Ratings: A-7.B-5.C-7.D-7.
Open: 11-2. Tel. 248 4062. Basic Cost £12 A/V/AE/DC.
Appearance: Staff young, very versatile & racially varied. One Spanish.
Car Parking: Park on premises at rear or on a nearby meter.
Ladies: 3 to 5 from 25 different. Facilities: Videos, Steam Room, Gym & Stoneroom.

VENUS AROMATHERAPY CLUB ☆☆☆
72, Sandyford Place Lane Ratings: A-5.B- .C-8.D-5.
Open: 11-12. Tel. 221 8722. Basic Cost £12.
Appearance: Staff young and versatile. One Chinese, one Thai.
Car Parking: Drive into lane & park nearby.
Ladies: 3 from 8 different. Facilities: Sauna & Videos.

WOODLANDS HEALTH SALON ☆☆☆☆
2, Woodlands Terrace Ratings: A-7.B- .C-9.D-6.
Open: Mon-Fri 11-10.Sat 11-6. Tel. 332 6337. Basic Cost £12.
Appearance: Staff presentable & racially varied, all ages, shapes & sizes.
Car Parking: Park on opposite side of the road if you can find a space.
Ladies: 4 from 7 different. Facilities: Sauna.

Part 3. Wales

CLWYD - FLINTSHIRE

To the west of Chester, in the north east corner of Wales are two lone parlours, neither of any great note. One occupies a nondescript shop in the middle of Shotton, the other the flat over a Tandoori restaurant on the outskirts of the small town of Bagillt, near Flint.

There is little else worth saying.

BAGILLT - 01352

FINESSE ☆☆☆
Over Little Bengal Tandoori Restaurant, High St. Ratings A-6.B- .C-9.D-6.
Open: 12-9. Tel. 710786. Basic Cost £10
Appearance: Staff white, youngish, cheerful, versatile & mainly busty.
Car Parking: At the north end of town by Holywell turn off. Park by the building.
Ladies: 1 from 7 different. Facilities: Fantasy Room.

DEESIDE - 01244

CONNECTIONS ☆☆☆
32, Chester Rd. East, Shotton Ratings:A-7.B- .C-7.D-6.
Open: 12-9. Tel. 813852 Basic Cost: £10.
Appearance: Staff young, versatile & racially varied inc. ladies from Italy & Brazil.
Car Parking: Park around the corner in Chester Close.
Ladies: 2 from 6 different. Facilities: Videos & Sunbed.

DYFED - CARMARTHENSHIRE

This rural corner of south west Wales is not a part of the country with which one would associate massage, but one parlour has recently opened in the old county town of Carmarthen. Discreetly located just west of the town centre, it is a pretty basic establishment, but then again could one expect any more here out in the sticks.

CARMARTHEN - 01267

CARMARTHEN MASSAGE ☆☆☆
Merlin Chambers, 104, Lammas St. Ratings: A-6.B- .C-7.D-5.
Open: Mon-Sat 11-8. Tel. 236667. Basic Cost £5.
Appearance: Staff racially varied, all ages, shapes & sizes.
Car Parking: Park outside or opposite.
Ladies: 2 from 10 different. Facilities: Videos.

GWENT

There used to be two parlours in Newport, Gwent, the only town in Newport to have any massage facilities. But unfortunately one has now closed and it was the better one of a poor selection. About what is left little of use can be said.

NEWPORT - 01633

STUDIO ONE ☆☆
107, Lower Dock St. Ratings:A-5.B- .C-8.D-5.
Open: 11-10. Tel. 216010. Basic Cost £10
Appearance: Staff young, white , versatile & all shapes & sizes.
Car Parking: Park opposite. Entrance confusingly through door marked 106.
Ladies: 2 from 10 different. Facilities:

MID-GLAMORGAN

Like Gwent and Dyfed, this county boast just one parlour, but at least this is one I can recommend. It lies in the market town of Bridgend roughly midway between Cardiff & Swansea. Tucked in a back street lies Body Talk, still with a confusing sign outside saying Oasis, indeed it also has recently had the name Dreams Health Club. One thing I have found on my travels is how parlours regularly seem to change name, but this one takes the cake.

The facilities include sauna, jacuzzi & videos and a charming workforce. I found myself greeted by the same lady on both occasions I visited it. Half Italian, she was charm itself.

BRIDGEND - 01656

BODY TALK ☆☆☆☆
1A, Merthyr Mawr Rd. Ratings:A-7.B- .C-8.D-6.
Open: 11-11. Tel. 645202 Basic Cost £10
Appearance: Staff white, young, presentable, versatile & charming.
Car Parking: Park along the road.
Ladies: 2 from 8 different. Facilities: Sauna, Jacuzzi & Videos.

SOUTH GLAMORGAN

South Glamorgan is essentially, for massage purposes anyway, Cardiff. And Cardiff has with the possible exception of Edinburgh the best quality parlours in the country. There are not that many of them - seven in all, but all of them are better than average with four 4-Star establishments and one 5-Star.

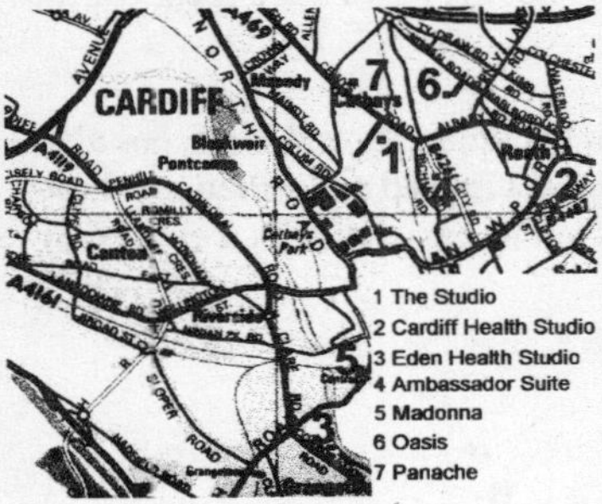

In a class on its own is The Studio. Located in the Cathays area of the city the establishment, only just opened, has first class decor and facilities, with a fully mirrored room, a fantasy room, as well as the usual sauna, jacuzzis and videos. Furthermore the staff are uniformly young, slim & attractive.

Left
VIP room
at the Studio

Right
The king size
Jacuzzi at the
Ambassador Suite

But there are other parlours with almost as good facilities. At Ambassador Suite in City Rd. if you would like a massage from a male Transvestite, that can be arranged. Furthermore the 25 different ladies working there, almost all uniformly young, slim & attractive, include ladies from China, Germany & Brazil. At Madonna in Penarth Rd., the slim international staff include ladies from Spain, Sweden, Hawaii & the Philippines, as well as some delightful local ladies.

Left
The Jacuzzi
Room at
Oasis

Right
The VIP
Room at
Madonna

Extreme versatility is the watchword at not only the Studio and Ambassador Suite, but also at Oasis. There the staff tend to be mainly Welsh but include some very attractive staff, though the one I found most tasty was perhaps slightly over made-up. The fantasy room there is not the best I have seen, but the staff more than make up for that.

Panache, which has recently moved from the premises next door, has also a distinctive range of ladies available but having just moved and still in the throes of adjusting to their new premises it difficult as yet to come up with a clear view of where they are heading.

CARDIFF - 01222

AMBASSADOR SUITE ☆☆☆☆
179A, City Rd. Ratings:A-7.B- .C-9.D-6.
Open: Sun-Thurs 10.30-4.30, Fri-Sat 10.30-7.30. Tel. 465970. Basic Cost £10.
Appearance: Staff racially varied, shapely, all sizes and ages and very versatile, including ladies from China, Brazil and Germany
Car Parking: Park by entrance at rear. Use alley off Northcote St.
Ladies: 4 from 25 different. Facilities: Sauna, Jacuzzi & Videos.

CARDIFF HEALTH STUDIO ☆☆☆
13A, Broadway, Roath Ratings:A-6.B- .C-7.D-6.
Open: 10.30-11. Tel. 493270. Basic Cost £5
Appearance: Staff cheerful, versatile, racially varied & all ages, shapes & sizes. Some of the ladies are very attractive.
Car Parking: Park outside.
Ladies: 3 from 20 different. Facilities: Sauna, Jacuzzi & Steam Room.

EDEN HEALTH STUDIO ☆☆☆
21, Corporation Rd. Ratings:A-6.B- .C-7.D-6.
Open: 10.30-1. Tel. 230666 Basic Cost £10.
Appearance: Staff youngish, racially varied & versatile.
Car Parking: Park outside or opposite.
Ladies: 3 from 12 different. Facilities: Sauna & Jacuzzi.

MADONNA ☆☆☆☆
17, Penarth Rd. Ratings:A-7.B- .C-5.D-7.
Open: 10.30-12. Tel. 229223 Basic Cost £10.
Appearance: Staff young, racially varied, versatile & mostly slim, inc. ladies from Sweden, Spain, Hawaii & the Philippines
Car Parking: Park opposite in Pay & Display by Central Rail Station.
Ladies: 4 from 20 different. Facilities: Jacuzzi & Videos.

OASIS ☆☆☆☆
39, Lochaber St., Roath Ratings:A-7.B- .C-8.D-7.
Open: Mon-Fri 10.30-11.Sat-Sun 11-11. Tel. 493311. Basic Cost £10.
Appearance: Staff mainly Welsh, young, white, presentable, very versatile & all shapes & sizes.
Car Parking: Park outside or nearby in Essich St. or Angus St.
Ladies: 3 from 12 different. Facilities: Sauna, Jacuzzi, Videos & Fantasy Room.

PANACHE ☆☆☆☆
140, Crwys Rd., Cathays Ratings:A-7.B-6.C-7.D-6.
Open: Sat-Thurs 10-12. Fri 10-2. Tel. 232203. Basic Cost A/V.
Appearance: Staff all ages, racially varied, very versatile & all shapes & sizes.
Car Parking: Park around the corner in Dogfield St.
Ladies: 3 from 15 different. Facilities: Sauna, Videos, Sunbed & Steam Room.

THE STUDIO ☆☆☆☆☆
112, Woodville Rd. Ratings: A-8.B- .C-9.D-8.
Open: Mon-Fri 10-2. Sat-Sun 10-4. Tel. 233482/236880. Basic Cost £10
Appearance: Staff young, all shapes & sizes, attractive & very versatile.
Car Parking: Park at rear in next door pub car park. Access off Basil Place.
Ladies: 4 from 12 different. Facilities: Sauna, Jacuzzis, Videos, Fantasy Room & Totally Mirrored Room.

WEST GLAMORGAN

The parlours of West Glamorgan are concentrated in Swansea, though there is one in nearby Briton Ferry. Four have closed down lately, and there certainly seems to be a high turnover of parlours in the Swansea area, though luckily that does not seem to apply to the three best parlours in the city.

The cream of the crop is Studio 95, only recently opened with first class decor, convenient parking at rear, acceptance of all major credit cards and first class facilities, including a king size jacuzzi & a brand new steam room. The staff, who often dress thematically, are predominantly local ladies but uniformly young & attractive.

A luxury massage room at Studio 95

The king size jacuzzi at Studio 95

But not far behind is Executive Health Club. It has been around a bit longer and consequently has not got Studio 95's advantage in fresh decor. However they are modernising the establishment and the basic cost of a massage is distinctly less. They also have a fully equipped fantasy room and accept all credit cards. Here again the staff are young & attractive.

Finally note should be made of Park Lane Club. While I could not get a basic price out of them, their facilities were extensive including a sunbed as well as the normal sauna and jacuzzi and the premises are very pleasantly decorated. When I visited it I found the establishment busy; the ladies mainly Welsh and young were not bad looking either.

NEATH - 01639

PARADISE CLUB ☆☆☆
99, Neath Rd., Briton Ferry Ratings:A-5.B- .C-7.D-6.
Open: Mon-Fri 11-10. Sat-Sun 12-8. Tel. 823269. Basic Cost £10.
Appearance: Staff young, white & versatile.
Car Parking: Park around the corner in Ritson St.
Ladies: 2 or 3 from 6 different. Facilities: Sauna & Jacuzzi.

SWANSEA - 01792

DIAMONDS ☆☆☆
72A, Ebenezer St. Ratings:A-6.B- .C-5.D-5.
Open: Mon-Fri 12-10. Sat-Sun 12-8. Tel. 455845. Basic Cost £5.
Appearance: Staff young, shapely, versatile & racially varied.
Car Parking: Park up the High St.
Ladies: 2 from 7 different. Facilities: Jacuzzi, Videos & Fantasy Room.

EXECUTIVE HEALTH CLUB ☆☆☆☆
22B, St. Helen's Rd. Ratings:A-7.B- .C-5.D-7.
Open: Mon-Sat 12-12. Sun 12-10.30. Tel. 456261. Basic Cost £5 A/V/AE/DC.
Appearance: Staff young, slim, versatile, racially varied & moderately attractive.
Car Parking: Park opposite up George St.
Ladies: 2 from 14 different. Facilities: Sauna, Jacuzzi, Videos & Fantasy Room.

MANHATTAN HEALTH CLUB ☆☆☆
57, Mansel St. Ratings:A-5.B- .C-8.D-6.
Open: 11-11. Tel. 456556 Basic Cost £2.
Appearance: Staff young, white & versatile. One half-Greek.
Car Parking: Park in front or at rear.
Ladies: 2 from 10 different. Facilities: Videos.

PARK LANE CLUB ☆☆☆☆
3, Ivey Place, High St. Ratings:A-7.B- .C-5.D-7.
Open: 10.30-4. Tel. 648195. Basic Cost
Appearance: Staff young, racially varied & mainly slim.
Car Parking: Park up the High St.
Ladies: 2 or 3 from 10 different. Facilities: Sauna, Jacuzzi, Videos & Sunbed.

STUDIO 95 ☆☆☆☆☆
95, Mansel St. Ratings:A-8.B- .C-9.D-8.
Open: 12-2. Tel. 467330. Basic Cost £25 A/V/AE/DC.
Appearance: Staff young, shapely, racially varied & attractive, including one lady from Italy.
Car Parking: Park at rear off alley off Verandah St.
Ladies: 4 from 28 different. Facilities: Sauna, Jacuzzi, Videos & Sunbed.

TOP CAT ☆☆☆
3, Humphrey St. Ratings:A-6.B- .C-6.D-7.
Open: Mon-Sat 11.30-10. Sun 1-8. Tel. 475366. Basic Cost £5.
Appearance: Staff youngish, white, versatile, cheerful & all shapes & sizes.
Car Parking: Park outside or elsewhere in the street.
Ladies: 2 from 6 different. Facilities: Videos.

PLEASE WRITE TO US

McCoy's Guides,
P.O.Box 243,
TELFORD,
Shropshire,
TF2 9WL

As I am sure you can appreciate, a lot of hard work and painstaking research has gone into the preparation of this book. Unfortunately I have not been able to give a B-rating , i.e. a mark for behaviour and performance, to many of the establishments.

As I tell the ladies working in these establishments as I travel around the country " If I had had a massage in each and every parlour that I have visited I would be worn out." However I have now begun to receive assistance from some of the readers of my first guide. I have been told of some parlours I have missed and have had some very interesting comments on my ratings for parlours I did cover.

More comments would indeed be much appreciated, particularly if you have had either particularly good or bad experiences. I can then bear these in mind, when preparing Guide No.3

My proposed Escort agency guide is going to take a little longer than I first thought, but provided I have your name and address and you respond favourably from time to time, we will be sending you details of further publications as they materialise.

Assuring you of my every best effort to keep you informed as to the value you can get in the adult entertainment industry,

I remain
yours faithfully

George McCoy

George McCoy

INDEX